"Prayer has never come easy to me, and there have been seasons when it has seemed impossible. I so want a life of prayer, but the possibility of prayer in the present moment often eludes me. In this book, my friend John Starke offers deep pastoral and biblical wisdom for those who want to answer God's invitation to prayer and to a deeper relationship with him."

Michael Wear, author of *Reclaiming Hope: Lessons Learned in the Obama White House About the Future of Faith in America*

"The information saturation and attention decay of the present moment can make prayer seem counterintuitive. In this book John Starke shows us how prayer has always been just that, a pull away from the ephemeral into the eternal. This book will show you the way to clearing your attention and your schedule in order to communicate with the One who loves you and holds your life together."

Russell Moore, president, the Ethics and Religious Liberty Commission of the Southern Baptist Convention

"If you find the idea of prayer impossible in today's hyperconnected world, you're not alone. But it's precisely this dilemma that makes *The Possibility of Prayer* such a powerful book. In this excellent volume, Starke explores how our established habits and daily rhythms will either make space for prayer or silence it before we even begin. With a pastor's heart, Starke then invites us, not simply to the act of prayer, but to lives of which prayer is a natural and necessary part."

Hannah Anderson, author of *Humble Roots: How Humility Grounds and Nourishes Your Soul*

"There are all sorts of reasons to praise *The Possibility of Prayer*: it is honest, rich, practical, realistic, deep, refreshing, sometimes poetic, and frequently profound. But the highest praise I can give it is that it did exactly what I'd hoped for—it helped me to pray. I am so grateful for John Starke, and for this book."

Andrew Wilson, teaching pastor, King's Church London

"*The Possibility of Prayer* is beautiful and deeply countercultural. John isn't asking us to layer another obligation on top of our lives but inviting us to a fundamental reorientation rooted in God's presence. Because John pastors a busy people in a busy city, he knows the cultural obstacles and the existential hurdles. But this is a profoundly hopeful and eminently practical book. What a gift this is to all of us!"

Chuck DeGroat, professor of pastoral care and Christian spirituality, Western Theological Seminary

"This is the kind of book we need right now. Starke doesn't just show us how to pray but how to form a life of prayer—and in turn, how prayer can form a life."

Justin Whitmel Earley, business lawyer at Earley Legal Group and author of *The Common Rule: Habits of Purpose for an Age of Distraction*

"Like anything worthwhile, a robust life of prayer does not come easily. Especially in our distracted age, we can throw in the towel on prayer before we even begin to explore the riches God has for us there. If you find yourself wishing that your prayers had more focus, more consistency, more zeal, more comfort, more fire—and more of God—John has provided a helpful, hopeful field guide for this worthy endeavor."

Scott Sauls, senior pastor of Christ Presbyterian Church, Nashville, author of *Jesus Outside the Lines* and *Irresistible Faith*

"What stands out above all about this book is its pastoral gentleness. You will look in vain in these pages for any judgmental tongue clucking about how dismal your prayer life probably is. Instead you will meet a fellow pilgrim eager to lead you to the rest—or better, to the One who gives rest and is himself rest—he has met in prayer."

Wesley Hill, associate professor of biblical studies, Trinity School for Ministry, Ambridge, Pennsylvania

"I've known and worked with John Starke for nearly a decade, and I can attest that he writes as he lives—as a man devoted to follow God from the depths of his heart. I've learned so much from watching him lead his family and church, and I learned even more through this penetrating new book. I didn't just glean from his experience or study; he helped me see more of God himself. And what greater need could any of us claim today?"

Collin Hansen, editorial director for The Gospel Coalition and author of *Blind Spots: Becoming a Courageous, Compassionate, and Commissioned Church*

"There few people I know who are as pastoral, thoughtful, and focused on transformative work as John Starke. This book reflects all of those values, making prayer feel accessible and urgent for our frenzied times. For those struggling to learn to pray, this is a timely and invaluable resource."

Mike Cosper, host of the *Cultivated* podcast and author of *Recapturing the Wonder*

"In *The Possibility of Prayer* John Starke has done something masterful. He has woven together a framework of the deep questions of prayer with its most compelling practices. Touching the mind, inspiring the heart, and rooted in formative practices, this book will indeed make that which seems impossible, possible, helping you become someone who lives and loves a prayerful life. Highly recommended!"

Jon Tyson, lead pastor, Church of the City New York, author of *The Burden is Light*

THE

POSSIBILITY

of PRAYER

FINDING STILLNESS WITH
GOD IN A RESTLESS WORLD

JOHN STARKE

An imprint of InterVarsity Press
Downers Grove, Illinois

InterVarsity Press
P.O. Box 1400, Downers Grove, IL 60515-1426
ivpress.com
email@ivpress.com

InterVarsity Press® is the book-publishing division of InterVarsity Christian Fellowship/USA®, a movement of students and faculty active on campus at hundreds of universities, colleges, and schools of nursing in the United States of America, and a member movement of the International Fellowship of Evangelical Students. For information about local and regional activities, visit intervarsity.org.

Scripture quotations, unless otherwise noted, are from The Holy Bible, English Standard Version, copyright © 2001 by Crossway Bibles, a division of Good News Publishers. Used by permission. All rights reserved.

While any stories in this book are true, some names and identifying information may have been changed to protect the privacy of individuals.

Published in association with the literary agent Don Gates of The Gates Group, www.the-gates-group.com.

Cover design and image composite: David Fassett
Interior design: Daniel van Loon
Images: watercolor collage: © Marthadavies / E+ / Getty Images
  rainy scene: © UygarGeographic / E+ / Getty Images
  sea and sand abstract: © Evgeniya Gaydarova / iStock / Getty Images Plus
  roses on blue background: © oxygen / Moment Collection / Getty Images
  white wood texture: © Wirat Namkate / EyeEm / Getty Images
  aerial view of modern buildings: © Scott Butterworth / EyeEm / Getty Images
  blue abstract watercolor: © Sergey Ryumin / Moment Collection / Getty Images
  watercolor background: © Sergey Ryumin / Moment Collection / Getty Images
  blue sky: © JuhyunMun / EyeEm / Getty Images
  blurred pastel color background: © eamanver / iStock / Getty Images Plus
  blue abstract watercolor background: © Sergey Ryumin / Moment Collection / Getty Images
  abstract watercolor: © Sergey Ryumin / Moment Collection / Getty Images
  oil painting texture: © Sergey Ryumin / Moment Collection / Getty Images
  green leaf: © Henri Uzo / EyeEm / Getty Images

ISBN 978-0-8308-4579-8 (print)
ISBN 978-0-8308-5000-6 (digital)

Printed in the United States of America ♾

InterVarsity Press is committed to ecological stewardship and to the conservation of natural resources in all our operations. This book was printed using sustainably sourced paper.

Library of Congress Cataloging-in-Publication Data
A catalog record for this book is available from the Library of Congress.

P	21	20	19	18	17	16	15	14	13	12	11	10	9	8	7	6	5	4	3	2	1
Y	38	37	36	35	34	33	32	31	30	29	28	27	26	25	24	23	22	21	20		

CONTENTS

INTRODUCTION

I WAKE UP WITH some effort at 5:30 a.m. and it's still dark. It is quiet, but that won't last long. The kids will be up soon, hustling to pour their Cheerios, comb each other's hair, throw their backpacks on, and make it out the door before the 1 Train comes to take us away to our day. But not yet. It is still quiet. Just me with my coffee.

The lists and notes scattered around my desk tempt me to start my day early. There's a lot to do today: people who need care, a sermon that needs attention, and a few meetings that require some thought. Those tasks call out: Come to me, all who are *anxious* and want to get stuff done! Don't you want to get stuff done? Yes, my heart says, yes! I want to get stuff done.

But not yet. There will be time for that soon. Not enough time, for sure, but time for it. Since there is never enough time,

I'm reminded that all I am, all I long for, all my hopes and plans can never be fulfilled and accomplished in time. Time always runs out and leaves me disappointed. My heart doesn't seem to accept the limitations that time offers. It has eternity pumping all the way through to the bottom. I need something more than just *enough* time.

I remember reading a book on how to best take advantage of all 168 hours of the week. Something in me wants to see each of those as opportunities to accomplish all that I want to get done and satisfy everyone I desperately do not want to disappoint. We crave glory and think we can pack it into 168 hours. No wonder there's never enough time. "Man is the creature with a mystery in his heart that is bigger than himself."[1] The mystery within isn't the problem; it's the context in which we try to work out the mystery that fails us. The inside is bigger than the outside.

Here is a spiritual peculiarity to explore: that eternity is what we crave, and the first thing our disillusioned brains think to do is cram it into the hours of the working week. I need something more than *enough* time—time management can't be the answer here. My notes and lists will have to wait.

I move from my desk to my chair in the corner. Psalm 141 helps me pray: "Let my prayer be counted as incense before you." Yes, that's a good way to begin: "incense before you." Like an aroma that provokes pleasure and satisfaction—that's what I want my prayers to be like.

But how can they? I am filled with inner conflicts. I am full of contradictions and mixed motivations. In Psalm 141 the psalmist will get to praying against his enemy, whoever that may be, but surely the psalmist is aware that there's at least a bit of the enemy in him. I know there is in me.

"Let my prayer be counted as incense before you." Let it be counted as something it inherently is not: a pleasing aroma. Do you see what the psalmist is doing here? It takes a slow reading sometimes to catch the word *counted*. David is asking that his prayers be seen as something they are not within themselves.

Break my prayers down to their essential elements, and you will find contradictory longings and desires. You will see cravings I am ashamed of. *What are these doing here?* If you poke around, you see repentance and hopes of reconciliation, but also cravings to be *right* in the eyes of others and to have an ease of conscience to just get along with my day without the nagging weight of sin hanging around.

Let me be washed—but is there an express lane?

A few mornings ago I read Psalm 138, which seems to begin with a running start: "I give you thanks, O LORD, with my whole heart." Whole heart? I look down at my coffee. What did David have for breakfast that gave him this whole-heart prayer? My prayers often feel at best halfhearted and distracted. Who can deliver me from my enemies, and who can deliver me from my prayers? Sitting in my old chair with fresh sins, let my prayers be counted worthy. Let my halfhearted prayers be counted as full-hearted.

Jesus tells me not to think my many words can beautify my prayers enough to be heard. Babbling—going on as if I can impress or charm the Almighty—is silly talk more than prayer. But my impulse to babble is a sign that my heart knows its shortcomings. My babbling is just my darkness talking, acting as an angel of light again. That won't work. It never works. It merely turns my prayers into court arguments and me into a court jester. But Jesus knows this temptation. He is a sympathetic priest who is acquainted with my weakness. "We can go together," he tells me. "That way you can enter with confidence to receive mercy and find grace to help in time of need." Quit your babbling, he tells me, and talk like a son.

My prayers will have to be reckoned as incense. Beauty will have to be a gift I receive by faith. My prayers will have to begin in the posture of reception, an active welcome. So here I am, in my worn-out chair with fresh grace again.

Now there's nothing left to do but enjoy this gift and tell him everything that's on my heart. Faith is believing that he enjoys it too. I have about half my coffee left and twenty minutes until the kids start stretching, but not yet. Eternity has visited and given me friendship and company.

I wonder if a book on prayer holds out only a frail hope for you. For many, a life of prayer and spiritual depth is not for them. It's not that they do not desire it; it's that they believe it is out of reach. There have been too many false starts in their spiritual life. A lot of well-intentioned declarations of commitment puttered to stalls and stops. Humming under the hood is the belief: *a deep and satisfying prayer life is not for me.*

Do you believe that? I want you to know it's not true.

Someone once told me that when she hears others talk about a life of prayer, she often thinks about someone else, someone in her church who seems to have his spiritual life together. A deep and satisfying prayer life always seems to be out of reach and not for her.

Here is what you should know and believe: a life of prayer, full of joy, power, and awe is for you. It's not for "other people." Prayer is not for the spiritually elite. It's for you.

Busyness is the first obstacle to prayer that people mention. I pastor a church in Manhattan, full of busy people. I once sat with a young mother who was a vice president at one of the major television networks in New York. She was working in a competitive field and had just given birth to her second child. The idea of spending time in prayer—something that she desired—seemed overwhelming and impossible. But she also knew that entering into a busy world, with the pressures of family and vocation, without some spiritual life seemed impossible.

But you don't need a baby or a highly demanding job to be tempted to crowd out prayer. Busyness is not a plague that only a few of us suffer from. It's the way of the world.

Busyness, however, isn't the deepest of our obstacles. Let's imagine we follow the instruction of Psalm 46:10: "Be still, and know that I am God." Just try it. Go ahead. Sit still. How long? Let's say ten minutes. Sit still for ten minutes and recognize his God-ness in your life. Which means that he's in control, not you, so you wait on him. Stillness. You don't conjure him up or manipulate what's going on: you seek to *know* him as God. Be still. If I sit still, I recognize how foreign this experience is to me. Normally, if I sit still, it is to accomplish something: I'm emptying out my inbox, writing a letter, listening to someone else tell a story, reading, or being entertained. Stillness before God is different. In stillness, intolerable things begin to happen.

One is guilt. An overwhelming sense that I ought to be doing something different, anything that is *accomplishing* something.

Does that surprise you? It has surprised me in the past. Prayer doesn't seem to be accomplishing the immediate. I am not being effective or efficient in prayer. It can seem like such a waste of time.

Anxiety then follows. Being active and busy is a good remedy for ignoring anxious thoughts. We stuff our fears down through activity. When I'm still, I'm suddenly vulnerable to all the things I've swept under the rug for so long. The monsters of insecurities and shame come home to me during the stillness of prayer. Busyness is good news for those of us who want to resist stillness like the plague. Busyness helps us avoid the ghosts and goblins of our fears and anxieties—but it cuts us off from healing as well.

We live in an age of efficiency. We judge our *use of time* by what we accomplish or produce. Anything we do that seems inefficient or unhurried is a *waste of time*. "I didn't get anything done today." If that's how we evaluate our use of time, is it any wonder we rarely justify the time for prayer, much less any meaningful spiritual exercise? A life with God calls for unhurried time that is driven not by accomplishments or tasks but by love and communion. Nothing is earned or achieved in prayer. God gives everything as a gift to those of us who are still and vulnerable enough to receive it.

But our age of pathological efficiency has taught our hearts to resist *any* moments of quiet, unhurried time. We fear the judgment of using our time inefficiently. You cannot prove your worth by your quiet prayers in secret.

The writer Oscar Wilde said, "Art is utterly useless."[2] Notice he did not say worthless. He was critiquing the utilitarian impulse of our world that measures worth based on usefulness or practicality. Does it accomplish something? Does it get stuff done? Wilde criticized a world that did not see art as valuable because they did not see its usefulness. Our modern world isn't much different. Art isn't practical; it doesn't give us tangible results. It rarely *earns* us anything.

Could this be part of why prayer is difficult for our modern world? Do we find prayer use*less* because it's not use*ful*? Maybe we've walked away from prayer and wondered, *Was that a good use of my time? Could I have gotten something done instead of praying? Do my prayers accomplish anything?*

The Bible challenges our utilitarianism. The prayers in the Psalms use words of waiting, watching, listening, tasting and seeing, meditating, and resting. It's remarkable how inefficient these actions are. They aren't accomplishing anything. There isn't a product on the other side of these prayerful actions. Yet over the years they bring steadfastness, joy, life, fruitfulness, depth of gratitude, satisfaction, wonder, an enlarged heart, feasting, and dancing.

We cannot merely say that the psalmist's life was just a different age. "Theirs was the life of pasture," we might say, "and ours is modern and metropolitan." The church's greatest examples of prayer and meditation are from King David—a man leading a young nation—or the prophet Elijah, who was often running for his life. Even St. Augustine lived a very active life as a bishop in the large and bustling town of Hippo, North Africa, in the fourth century. His life was full of regular pastoral duties, travel, theological controversies, and the constant threat of military invasion from enemies. Even more, in a span of forty years his writing output would equal a thick three hundred-page book a year. And yet he maintained that this resulted from long and regular times of prayer and solitude with God.

A deeper look into biblical patterns of prayer and ancient rhythms of solitude reveals an overwhelming witness that the contemplative life is not just for the hermit, the priest, or the desert monk, but for the banker, the mother, and the artist. In fact, the contemplative life is for all of life, for every vocation, and for every village, town, and city.

The witness of Christian history is that the ambitious need quiet hearts. We need ancient paths for our modern, busy lives that teach us to be settled with God in an unsettling world.

The rhythms of our world do not make space for the habits of prayer: Communion, meditation, solitude, fasting and feasting, Sabbath rest, and corporate worship. We are in danger of being formed by our calculating age of technique and efficiency, rather than the quiet Voice that forms us when we are with him.

In Psalm 81 the Lord reminds his people how he has delivered them and how he will sustain them.

I am the LORD your God,
    who brought you up out of the land of Egypt.
    Open your mouth wide, and I will fill it. (Psalm 81:10)

Prayer is the daily habit of opening your mouth wide for all the fullness of God.

PART 1

THE POSSIBILITY *of* PRAYER

A VIBRANT PRAYER LIFE is possible for you. I know it may not seem this way, but the whole thing is rigged for triumph.

That doesn't mean that prayer will be easy or comfortable. It won't. In fact, we should prepare for the long, slow haul of discomfort, confusion, and frustration, laced with joy, love, stability, and wholeness. There aren't a few techniques merely to pick up so that next week the struggle for prayer will be over. Instead, there are realities that we need to grasp that lead to *pathways* (rather than techniques) toward intimacy with God. These realities—like the incarnation of Christ, our participation in Christ's exalted status, and his participation in our troubled and lowly place—rearrange how we think about ourselves, God, and the world around us.

This often means unlearning lies about ourselves, God, and the world that have driven how we've lived and made decisions so far in our lives. That will take time because it's not merely changing our minds or our perspectives but *growing up into* who we are in Christ and *embodying* the truth. Like a child maturing into adulthood, this doesn't happen after learning about adulthood, but by growing up into it and slowly putting on its characteristics.

However, maturity and grasping true reality are not the only struggles in a life of prayer. Anxiety, pain, loss, boredom, guilt, and sin take swings at our spiritual lives that often make prayer seem impossible and quiet moments intolerable. We deal with these by distancing ourselves from the potential presence of God, closing down our openness but shutting out the healing. However, prayer is possible, even in pain; intimacy is available, even for the anxious.

Maneuvering through these various hindrances takes wisdom and patience, but God provides everything we need in the time that we need it. Prayer helps us see those provisions. So the first part of this book is about *why* prayer is possible. It's possible because God has made it possible, and his provisions are more powerful than our hindrances.

CHAPTER ONE

THE IMPOSSIBILITY OF PRAYER

THE CRAB NEBULA is an exploding star about forty-two hundred light years away. I first learned about it in Annie Dillard's *Teaching a Stone to Talk*. Light from this exploding star first became visible to earth in 1054. It was a supernova then, so bright it could be seen during the daytime. A thousand years later, the star is still exploding.

What explodes for a thousand years? What has the density and size to keep up this pace?

If you look at the Crab Nebula today through binoculars, it looks like a little ring. If you stare at it, even with earnest stillness, you will see no movement. The naked eye clothed with binoculars looks at this exploding star, and it seems more like a statue. "Photographs of the Crab Nebula taken fifteen years ago seem identical to photographs of it taken yesterday," and yet the Crab

Nebula is expanding at the rate of seventy million miles a day, and it's been doing that for millennia.[1]

We are in a universe where something that has increased in size by over a billion miles wide over a fifteen-year period goes unnoticed. Currently, I am sitting in an apartment in the northeast corner of the United States, which is on a planet that is 1.5 billion times larger than my body. The Crab Nebula expands twenty-nine hundred times larger than earth *every* day. And yet it is a fairly small blip in the grand scheme of schemes. Why is it a fairly small blip? Because before now chances are this is the first time you have given much sustained thought to this wonder of light and beauty. The Crab Nebula is a constantly expanding firework that lights up whole corners of the universe, and for hundreds of years, anyone conscious enough to give attention has not given it much attention at all.

It is false humility to call ourselves a speck in the universe. Put your hand over your mouth (Job 21:5) and consider that the exploding Crab Nebula is a speck. What are we?

Looking at a picture of the Crab Nebula, we see its astonishing beauty. But realize that its light pushes out thousands and thousands of light years away, and we begin to grasp how much of the beauty we do not sense. Star worship is ungodly, but the Crab Nebula proves that the temptation is not unreasonable.

Who is this God of exploding stars, and what have we to do with him? God is infinitely larger than this light god that's expanding seventy million miles a day, and God's glory is more majestic than this speck pushing its light to anything that can see, thousands of light years away. And we have a universe full of Crab Nebulas, their glory shining from end to end.

Somehow humans have pondered the idea of communicating with this God of exploding stars. Did we inherit this insanity? Are we sure we want to call upon this Being to give attention to us? He blew up the Crab Nebula and sends the warning flares of his exploding power for any being conscious enough to see for thousands of light years in every direction. He is not gentle with specks, so how do we know he will be gentle with us? The Crab Nebula is a witness to us who ponder prayer, "Beware! This is a possibility!"

Recently, a man drove onto a sidewalk in lower Manhattan and plowed over a group of cyclists and then got out and shot more. Eight were killed in a moment, and several more injured. We lamented this tragedy on Sunday morning at our church. A room full of people gathered in the morning and evening and asked God why. We wept and prayed.

The death of a star causes beauty and wonder for billions of miles all over the universe for thousands of years, and the universe shrugs. *Our* death produces a pile of ash, and we demand the attention and explanation of the divine. And isn't this explosion a witness to a pattern of the universe: destruction and chaos rather than care and mindfulness? Who wept for the Crab Nebula? Who has taught us to weep rather than shrug? Worse, where does our arrogance come from that we are offended at the God of exploding specks when things go terribly wrong?

Many philosophers and public intellectuals have suggested that humans would experience new freedom if we would evolve past this irrational self-importance and just live. "Perhaps it's ridiculous to take ourselves so seriously," says Thomas Nagel.[2] Live and shrug. As Alison Gopnik puts it,

Ultimately, the metaphysical foundations don't matter. Experience is enough all by itself. What do you lose when you give up God or "reality" or even "I"? The moon is still just as bright; you can still predict that a falling glass will break, and you can still act to catch it; you can still feel compassion for the suffering of others. Science and work and morality remain intact. Go back to your backgammon game after your skeptical crisis, Hume wrote, and it will be exactly the same game.

In fact, if you let yourself think this way, your life might actually get better. Give up the prospect of life after death, and you will finally really appreciate life before it. Give up metaphysics, and you can concentrate on physics. Give up the idea of your precious, unique, irreplaceable self, and you might actually be more sympathetic to other people.[3]

Yet, despite the witness of the Crab Nebula and even the encouragement of some of our philosophers, Christians have sought to pray to this God and seek his comfort, wisdom, love, forgiveness, attention, and help. We seek to know this God of exploding stars and trust that though he is dangerous, he is good and loves us. Christians believe that God is not only mindful of our trouble, but he desires to give us glory and pleasure in himself.

Prayer is either the greatest insanity or the most wonderful news.

Prayer is calling on God for his attention. We ask him to turn away from the exploding stars and supernovas and give attention to our trouble. We ask him to show us mercy. Why would we think this is a good idea?

There are many explanations for why we have the confidence to pray. But the place to begin is the doctrine of the incarnation of God. God, in history, put on our humanity. Jesus Christ was not only a man but God. He was the God-man, as Christians have called him. He is God-come-to-us—to be with us and to *become* us. Anyone deciding to pick up the vocation of prayer needs to be newly and deeply aware that something impossible has happened: God, in his absolute being, has resolved to make himself known and seen and felt and touched in human life.

Prayer is not possible because we have somehow made ourselves worthy of God's attention, but because God has made himself known to us. We did not have to ascend like phoenixes out of our ashes to get God's attention, but God descended into the depths of dust with us.

In the first century, Ignatius of Antioch wrote in a letter,

> There is only one God,
> revealed by Jesus Christ his Son,
> who is his Word sprung from silence.[4]

Jesus is the Word sprung from silence and put in flesh. Here is the mystery that we all should taste and see: Other religions create programs for men and women to purify themselves, to be worthy enough, or to be one with the divine. We must transcend our existence, they tell us, to be with God, to reach God, to be worthy of God. We must put off our flesh, our humanity, our weakness, our passions, and reach for God. And if we are elite and spiritual enough, God reaches back. But Jesus is the God who came down. He condescended to be with us. He put on *our* flesh, *our* humanity, *our* weakness and took hold of us. He experienced our humanity that we might experience his glory.

This is almost sheer madness. If the difference between us and God is as terrible as the exploding Crab Nebula suggests, which is the more reasonable way? That humans transcend their insignificant existence and try to become great enough, holy enough, worthy enough for the God of exploding stars to give attention to? Or that God, in his love, made himself lowly enough for us to know and embrace him?

Either we must put on divinity or he must put on humanity. Which is more reasonable? Both seem like madness, but only one is good news.

Annie Dillard attended a small congregation in a town in Northwest United States. The singing was awkward and the preaching was boring. *Is this the kind of worship and proclamation the God of exploding stars deserves?* she wonders. Come to think of it, is any worship and proclamation of any church worthy of him?

A high school stage play is more polished than this service we have been rehearsing since the year one. In two thousand years, we have not worked out the kinks. We positively glorify them. Week after week we witness the same miracle: that God is so mighty he can stifle his own laughter. Week after week, we witness the same miracle: that God, for reasons unfathomable, refrains from blowing our dancing bear act to smithereens. Week after week Christ washes the disciples' dirty feet, handles their very toes, and repeats, It is all right—believe it or not—to be people. Who can believe it?[5]

The Incarnation is the way God has come close to us. Jesus lived on earth, as God and man, serving, eating, drinking, talking, sleeping, and dying. He was weak and needed strength. He was tempted in every way we are and yet, in a very human way, found power in the Spirit to resist. He rested and prayed. He feasted and wept. He spoke truth and defended the poor. In fact, he was poor—homeless, at times. In other words, he didn't just have a "human experience," as someone who visits London for the weekend has a "very British experience." He *was* human. Immanuel. God with us.

When we are going through trouble or pain, we're tempted to wonder at how God could understand our trouble, our pain, our loss. How could he? He's perfect and never needs anything! How many prayers begin with, "But God, you just don't understand!" God can grasp complex formulas and has an encyclopedic knowledge of the universe—but does he know my pain?

The incarnation of God teaches us to see differently. A god who cannot comprehend our pain or understand our trouble is a false god. The God of Jesus Christ knows what it means to be poor, to be troubled in spirit, to suddenly lose his best friend to death, to be falsely accused, to be slandered, to be abandoned by his closest companions, to be misunderstood by family, to be mocked, ashamed, humiliated, and hated. He knows what it means to face death. In the incarnation, "God becomes our neighbor."[6]

Here's the deeper mystery: when Jesus died and rose again, he arose not as an angel or as something else more than human. He was resurrected as a man with a body, glorified and new. When he ascended to the heavens, his body didn't just slip off as he rose past the clouds. He was resurrected, fully man and fully God, and he has made himself available to us by his Spirit. As the old church fathers used to say, the resurrected and ascended Christ lets us pray "as his contemporary." He becomes our neighbor and friend, our companion and our intimate.

The mystery of our faith is that God is at the same time *beyond* us, *with* us, and *in* us.

The witness of the incarnation, Christ's suffering, and the resurrection point us to a deeper data of how to think about prayer than the evidence we see in the universe. Exploding stars and the suffering of violence are only partial evidence. We are tempted to believe a shrug is more reasonable than our desire for God's attention and mercy.

But somehow God does not shrug. Instead, the life and sufferings of Christ, the Son of God, give us deeper evidence of God's participation with us—that God is present in our world. We may not be able to fully explain the presence of evil and suffering, but the answer cannot be that God shrugs. The weeping, suffering, and dying Christ won't let us give that answer.

And so Christians have prayed. Jesus commands us to. He tells us to pray God *into* our trouble, and in exchange we enter his joy.

In Matthew 9, Jesus is having a meal with a disreputable crowd. "Tax collectors and sinners," they were called. Tax collectors have always had less-than-appealing profiles among us, but this was more menacing. Tax collectors were traitors to the first-century Jewish communities. They were Jews who were working for the Roman government, an oppressive regime, to gather and collect tyrannical taxes. They were the enforcers and often took more for their own pockets. They were working for the ruling powers who defiled their temples.

The Gospel of Matthew tells us that Jesus was "reclining" with them. He feasted and found friendship. The religious leaders found out about this dinner and thought this was out of bounds for a teacher like Jesus, and they rebuked Jesus and his disciples for it.[7]

Jesus responded, "Those who are well have no need of a physician, but those who are sick. Go and learn what this means, 'I desire mercy and not sacrifice.' For I came not to call the righteous, but sinners" (Matthew 9:12-13).

Let's follow the words of Jesus to "go and learn" what this means.

I was looking at an old journal in which I had written some reflections on this passage. I concluded that I ought to be more ready to spend time with those who may cause me to feel uncomfortable or out of place because they have different values and lifestyles. I need to be friends with people Jesus was friends with and eat with people Jesus ate with.

Of course, that is a perfectly legitimate implication of the story, but it's a disastrous first step. The first question in reading stories like this is not, What did Jesus do and how do we do it? but What does Jesus offer and how do we put ourselves in a position to receive it? Jesus is trying to get us to see not who we need to be befriending but what we need to be in order for Jesus to befriend us! And, of course, Jesus befriends the sick and needy.

My initial reading of the story put me above the needy and sick. It made me a *helper* of the sick, a *friend* of sinners, not a sick sinner myself. Without realizing it, I read the text to affirm what I obviously believed and lived, all the while feeling very virtuous. Who wouldn't want to be known as "helper of the sick" and "friend of sinners"?

Here is the first step of prayer in a universe where God has put on flesh to be with us: we must put ourselves in the way of his friendship to sick and needy sinners. The heart naturally resists this posture and disposition. If we see ourselves as healthy and self-sufficient, invulnerable and spiritually impressive, we will miss Jesus' healing and friendship. "Go and learn what this means," he says. It takes time and honest observation of our hearts.

Jean Vanier once told a community who lived and served the mentally disabled in Trosly, France, "Jesus did not say, 'Blessed are those who serve the poor,' but 'Blessed are the poor.'" Vanier said that if we want to sustain a long-term ministry to people who experience a kind of poverty that many will never experience, we must become poor ourselves.[8] It's a vocation that will garner us no praise or thanks. We will be forgotten and overlooked. The mentally disabled these people were serving didn't have the capacity, most of the time, to express thanksgiving or praise for the help they received.

Henri Nouwen reflected on Vanier's words by saying, "It is the way to poverty. Not an easy way, but God's way, the way of the cross."[9] If I'm poor and sick, then serving the poor and sick looks more like solidarity and friendship than condescension or benevolence.

"Blessed are you who are poor," Jesus said (Luke 6:20). That's a tough pill to swallow. If that seems confusing or a step too strange for you, it could be that you need patience with this instruction of Jesus. I would encourage you not to move past this too quickly. "Go and learn what this means," Jesus says. Resist the urge to move on.

It is a blessing to serve the poor. But Jesus tells us there is a deeper blessing that's a step or two before that: To be poor is the place of happiness. To need what Jesus has to give. To be in the posture of reception to his healing. Here is the beginning place of prayer: neediness, ready for blessedness.

Our modern world often sees our neighbors, relationships, marriages, religion, family, and civic engagements as enhancements, like a gym membership to enhance bodily health. Things that previous societies might have seen as obligations, we see as enhancements. They are meant to add and benefit, but the minute they begin to require sacrifice, become difficult, or challenge our assumptions, we move on. They aren't enhancing anymore.

Many of us see God like that. And so we think of prayer, too, as an enhancement. But if we take the posture characteristic of what the New Testament calls us toward—poor and needy for him—then our prayers will begin to take a deeper turn.

Just as Jesus says, "Blessed are you who are poor, for yours is the kingdom of God," so we can say, "Blessed are the sick sinners, for theirs is friendship with Jesus." Matthew says that Jesus "reclined" with sinners and tax collectors. It's an image of intimacy and friendship, of letting down your guard. I long for this kind of friendship, I just don't long for feeling needy.

If I'm needy, I'm out of control. I'm not in control of my reputation, and I'm at the mercy of Jesus. But his arms are everlasting arms. I can trust them. It is a good friendship. I am learning that it takes time to see how sick and poor I truly am, and it takes time to learn how trustworthy his friendship truly is.

You have kept count of my tossings;

>   put my tears in your bottle.

Are they not in your book? (Psalm 56:8)

I often resist bringing my troubles to God because I just don't want to think about them. They are burdensome for a reason, and it's easier to keep them compartmentalized and stuffed down. But with that comes needless burden carrying. And when I don't cast my own cares upon him, I can't carry the burdens of others.

"You have kept count of my tossing." I can imagine here the Lord watching and counting over me as I toss at night. Why do we toss? I suppose it's our body giving witness to the restlessness of our hearts. The Lord watches over this. It isn't exciting work; I'm sure exploding stars are more interesting, but he's interested. He gathers my tears and takes note of all my trouble.

He keeps count of my tossing just as he keeps count of my hairs. I don't think there are any narcissists in the world who love themselves enough to give attention to the detail of how many hairs are on their head—but God loves us that much. And it's not just impersonal facts about us that God keeps track of—the psalm makes clear that he doesn't stop there. He counts my tossing, gathers my tears, and makes notes about my trouble in his book. He's mindful and watching. He counts *one, two, three, four* . . . This is his work of presence with me. He notices and loves me.

I don't count my own tossing. When my wife asks me how I slept, I don't answer with how many times I tossed and turned, nor do I pay much attention to my tears other than to wipe them away. But he notices. If he knows these things, how much more does he know my trouble?

This is the universe we live in, where exploding stars that expand at the rate of seventy million miles a day can go unnoticed and unregistered to human beings, but where God keeps count of my tossing and gathers my tears. Who can believe it?

Now we are ready. We are in a universe made for prayer and perfect for beginners. Yes, principalities and powers tempt us to resist, and we have habits and muscle memories that keep us distracted and fearful of quiet. "Teach us to pray," Jesus' disciples asked him.

There is much to learn, but it's easy to get started.

CHAPTER TWO

THE PLACES OF PRAYER

WHEN MY FAMILY FIRST MOVED to New York, we lived in an apartment that had a little space between the kitchen and the dining room. We called it "the nook." I prayed there before everyone else got up. There was a comfortable chair, a bookshelf above my head, and a window that looked out to the city, twenty-one stories up. I could see the sunrise over the park and a number of bridges across the East River. It was a quiet corner, and at the time I thought it was one of the best places in all of New York City. If I'm honest, I still do.

Since then, our family has moved on to other apartments, and I've had to find my way into other nooks and corners, other places of stillness and retreat. In every apartment and home, I've had *some* place. But nothing was like that nook.

Over the years I've come to see how important a *place* of prayer is for me. Maybe it is for you as well. My life seems to flourish when there's a rhythm. If I have a *place* where I know I am going to be in the morning, it's one less thing to think about. I can be at home in that place. There's less fidgeting and more praying. I've ground my coffee the night before and set it up for when I wake up. When I'm up, I pour some coffee and settle in. Let's make this as uncomplicated as possible.

You and I are probably different in a million ways. Maybe you thrive on far more spontaneity than I do. My wife does. (I could maybe do with a little more spontaneity.) But I imagine we all need rhythms and a common place of prayer more than we think. We need a nook. We need a meeting place where we know we can give attention to one thing and not a dozen small things.

For you, maybe a window would take you to faraway places, and while that's wonderful for daydreaming, it distracts focused prayer. Maybe you need a plain, small room. Jesus tells us to find a prayer closet to pray (Matthew 6:6). The language he uses is about a room in the center of the house—a room without windows peeking in from the outer world—something like a food pantry. His concern is that we don't pray to show off our righteousness to the world, but some sideways wisdom could also be that praying in a closed space can keep us from seeing the whole world when we ought to only be seeing Jesus.

Maybe early mornings feel impossible. You work late or you're a morning monster, and for the sake of neighborly welfare you wonder if evening prayers are better. But let me give witness to what I have seen: many a friend has sought to pray later in the day because mornings seemed so hard, but they never sustained any regular habit of it. I'm sure there are any number of reasons why they didn't keep up with a regular afternoon prayer life, but

I imagine one of the most common was that once the day began, it was hard to pause the momentum of efficiency and productivity for stillness. To this I say (I, not the Lord), it may be wise to make your time of prayer in the mornings after all.

Morning or evening, you need a rhythm and a daily place of concentrated time, where efficiency and productivity do not have dominion. You need a place where the coffee or tea is hot, and all you have to do is sit and turn on the lamp. Make provisions for yourself. You need it. Nooks and rhythms are building blocks of a vibrant spiritual life.

If you have your nook and rhythm in place, and the dozens of small *other* things are out of your mind, let me focus your attention on the deeper place of prayer. Here's the basic assumption that the spiritual giants of Scripture and Christian history seem to have about prayer: Christ is personally and really present with us when we pray. I am sure you know that God is always present everywhere. We can take that for granted. But in an attentive, covenantal way, Christ is present with us in prayer.

The apostle Paul writes that God "raised us up with [Christ] and seated us with him in the heavenly places" (Ephesians 2:6). Both verbs are past tense. God *has raised* us and *has seated* us with Christ. In the small, hidden places where we attempt to be quiet and pray, we are raised with Christ and seated with him. We are simultaneously in our nooks and raised and seated with Christ in the heavenly places. The view from there is seen with the eyes of our hearts (Ephesians 1:16-19).

Take a deep breath and pause for a moment. Maybe read the previous paragraph again, gathering up all the wonder of what's been said so far: you are seated in your nook and seated with Christ, raised with him to the heavenly places. Christ was raised from the dead and ascended into heaven, bodily and truly after the resurrection. His ascension was his enthronement, where he was seated with power and glory. Now Paul is saying, "Look! In Christ, you also are raised and seated in glory!"

I don't want the small, fidgeting things to distract me from that place. I am seated with Christ; don't distract me with coffee filters! I don't want to try to find a comfortable place to sit, figuring out if the lighting is okay, when I have all the riches of Christ in the heavenly places to enjoy. Do we know what we have and what we are invited into when we pray? Let's not be asleep to what we're doing and where we are.

We need to be purposely aware of this reality with Christ because of our lack of intentional looking, longing, and praying for God's powerful presence with us only depletes our experience of it. Without that intentional recognition of his presence, prayer can seem distant and impersonal. Without the conscious welcome of his company (since he has welcomed ours), communion can often feel about as intimate as email.

In prayer we experience being raised and seated with Christ in the heavenly places. But what kind of God are we encountering there? What kind of being is he?[1] In the Bible we find a number of God's characteristics. We see God as *heavy, holy, joyful, beautiful, relational,* and *available*.

God as heavy. The Hebrew word for "glory" literally means *heavy*. The Bible intentionally contrasts the weightiness of God with the weightlessness of everything else in this world. "Heaven and earth will pass away," Jesus says, "but my words will not pass away" (Matthew 24:35). "To say that God is heavy is to recognize the intensity and the density of the reality of the divine being, in comparison with which the things of creation are but wisps or vapor or dreams."[2] "The mountains melt like wax before the LORD," the psalmist writes, "before the Lord of all the earth" (Psalm 97:5).

On our honeymoon, my wife and I drove through the Sierra Nevada to get to Lake Tahoe. As we slowly made our way through a chain of cathedrals thousands of feet high, dwarfing our little existences, we had to constantly stop to look and catch our breath. Mountains make us feel small. But the psalm tells us that these giant immovable bodies of rock, pushing up through cloud and sky, melt like wax before the presence of God.

As modern people we have natural impulses to think large thoughts of ourselves and small thoughts of God, which do not match his eternal and intense existence. Our thoughts of ourselves and of God do not match the reality.

When we pray, we come with Christ into the mountain-melting presence of God. He is more intensely and densely *real* than anything else. This is not a god of religious experiences or a god to be manufactured for trivial comfort. He is ultimate reality. He is the God of all being. He is the God who confronts Moses at the burning bush, saying, "Take your sandals off your feet, for the place on which you are standing is holy ground. . . . I AM WHO I AM" (Exodus 3:5, 14).

I am who I am. Pure and eternal being. He is not who we want him to be. *He is.* He is heavy, not light; he is not malleable to our desires for a human-sized divinity. He just *is.* If our natural impulse is to imagine ourselves as heavy with importance and God as light, prayer is the great reversal of our imagination.

God as holy. The prophet Isaiah tells of his experience before the throne room of God in Isaiah 6. The Lord was sitting on the throne, "the train of his robe filled the temple" (v. 1). Above the Lord were seraphim, flying with a set of six wings each. The six wings had practical uses. One set was used to fly, of course. Another was used to cover their faces. The last set was used to cover their feet. Attempts to paint these strange beings haven't always matched the sense of importance these seraphim carry. The image is almost absurd when we focus on the seraphim. But we aren't meant to focus on the seraphim; they're there to say something very serious about God.

Let's begin with their feet. In ancient Israelite culture, feet were seen as immodest when exposed. So to be in the presence of such a being as the Lord on his throne, the feet would need to be covered. Their faces were covered because of the terrifying gaze of the *weighty* One. To be in his presence was enough to provoke strange activity. They cried out, back and forth to one another, "Holy, holy, holy is the LORD of hosts; the whole earth is full of his glory!" (v. 3).

"Holy, holy, holy." What are they saying? Have you ever wondered that? What does that mean? Many people have tried to understand what God's holiness means. Some describe it as his perfect morality. God's holiness means he is sinless and untouched by corruption, which of course is true. But do you imagine the angels essentially crying out, "Moral, moral, moral is the LORD of hosts!" That doesn't quite seem to capture what's happening. It seems to domesticate it a bit, doesn't it?

Others have tried to explain it through the category of the "complete Other"—that God is Creator, eternal, but we are not. We are creatures, finite in our being. The Bible seems to say over and over and over that there is no one like God, no one beside him, no equal in worth, being, and power. Yes, we must agree, God is the God of *otherness*. But when we then imagine again our seraphim singing "Other, other, other," something is still missing.

When the Bible seeks to explain God's holiness, it says that God is a "consuming fire" (Exodus 24:17; Deuteronomy 4:24; Hebrews 12:29)—a dangerous and terrible presence. The presence of not just a fire that warms our hands and charms our campsites, but a consuming fire. Turn away! And so the angels do.

When Isaiah encounters this God, he cries out, "Woe is me! For I am lost;" (Isaiah 6:5). Translations differ: "I am lost!" or "I am undone!" or "I am ruined!" Something is coming apart in Isaiah in the presence of God. Yet, at the same time, Isaiah and the seraphim don't flee the terrible presence. The danger is real, but obviously so is the splendor. So terrifying and attractive, so immense and wonderful is God. So much so, when God is looking for someone to go to his people on his behalf, Isaiah says, "Here I am! Send me" (v. 8).

God as joyful. Who is like this God? Holy and heavy, yet joyful in his very essence. God takes joy in himself (John 17) and in his people (Proverbs 8:30-31; Zephaniah 3:17; Luke 15:5).

It may sound a little strange that God takes joy in himself— but we are entering the land of divine joy, so we ought to expect something strange and unfamiliar. In John 17, Jesus and his disciples are sitting at a table. It's the last moments before he is arrested and eventually led to his crucifixion. After some teaching, he begins to pray to the Father. His prayer both looks into a deeper reality of God and invites us in to experience it.

In this prayer Jesus recollects all the glory and delight and joy he has with the Father from all eternity. Jesus, the eternal Son, and the eternal Father have been in rich communion and delight unceasing. Jesus is pulling back the curtain from eternity past to reveal that the Father and the Son never experienced loss or lack, only delight and fullness in one another. The Father, the Son, and the Holy Spirit have been only in the complete fullness of joy and glory. Can you imagine? Just eternity and joy between them.

Then the prayer takes an unimaginable turn. Jesus begins to pray that we, his followers, would be brought into that delight. Jesus says, "Just as you, Father, are in me, and I in you, [I ask] that they also may be in us" (John 17:21). "The glory that you have given me I have given them" (v. 22). "I made known to them your name, and I will continue to make it known, that the love with which you have loved me may be in them, and I in them" (v. 26).

The invitation of Jesus is, "Share in my joy!" (see Matthew 25:23). Prayer is our daily yes to that invitation.

God as beautiful. "Worship the LORD in the splendor of holiness," the psalmist instructs us (Psalm 96:9). Holiness is mentioned again, but here the focus is its beauty. Interestingly, in the Old Testament, when God visits his people, it is often in the form of fire. Remember the burning bush (Exodus 3)? But even before that, in Genesis 15, when God makes a covenant with Abraham concerning the promise of his son, he comes down in the form of a blazing fire. He leads the Israelites through the wilderness to the Promised Land in the form of fire by night. The terrible presence of holiness on Mount Sinai showed itself as fire—both dangerous and beautiful. Gazing at fire causes wonder, although we must relate to it on its own terms.

"Worship the Lord in the [beauty] of holiness." Invitation and danger; danger and absolute bliss.

> One thing have I asked of the Lord,
> that I will seek after:
> that I may dwell in the house of the Lord
> all the days of my life,
> to gaze upon the beauty of the Lord
> and inquire in his temple. (Psalm 27:4)

One thing that all mature Christians agree on is the absolute beauty of God. They've experienced it! They've seen it and have been changed by it. They long for it, just like the writer of Psalm 27. "One thing I ask"—what is that one thing? To seek and to see the beauty of God. That's not a bad summary of prayer.

But that's not all. There's a running theme in the New Testament that beholding the beauty of God beautifies the beholder. In 2 Corinthians 3, Paul begins to explain that in Moses' day there was a veil, so to speak, over people's hearts in seeing the glory of God. But through Christ that veil is taken away for us (vv. 14-16). So now there is a way through prayer, reading Scripture, and worship to see the glory of God in Christ with an unveiled face. "And we all, with unveiled face, beholding the glory of the Lord, are being transformed into the same image from one degree of glory to another" (v. 18). There is a kind of looking, beholding, tasting, and seeing the glory and beauty of God that has a transformative effect on the lookers. We are changed from one degree to the next into that same glory and beauty.

When Christ finally and fully appears, "we shall be like him." Why? "Because we shall see him as he is" (1 John 3:2). We shall see him and be like him. Beauty has transformative power. Have you ever noticed that whether it comes from music, a painting, or a face, beauty affects us? It can lighten our faces and cause us to sigh with delight. Just a little bit, it beautifies us.

But the beauty of Christ is something more. It comes and completely transforms us, all the way down. No one else is like this. No one else has this sort of transformative power in their beauty. Christ's beauty is perfect and eternal, and it's ours to seek and to see.

God as relational. From all eternity God has been in joyful communion, the Father with the Son and with the Spirit. But the joy is *communion* joy, a relationship of delight. God has not merely made himself available to be seen, worshiped, and enjoyed, but to be known and loved.

A sad reality for many Christians is that their experience of God is rarely personal and relational. Maybe we have meaningful encounters in public worship or corporate prayer meetings, but intimacy has evaded our experience of him. The Father, Son, and Holy Spirit reality is a person-in-relationship reality. This is God's way of being, and he's inviting us into it—to commune with him and experience all the beauty and joy in person. Our relationship with God takes on the characteristic of how the Father relates to the Son. The potential for joy and ecstasy is infinite. And of course, the potential to miss it is heartbreaking.

God as available. Here is the confidence of the Psalms: the Lord is available to us. "O LORD, you hear the desire of the afflicted; you will strengthen their heart; you will incline your ear"

(Psalm 10:17). Our confidence is that he is not distracted from our needs, our pain, our longings. He is listening, looking, and waiting. "I call upon you, for you will answer me, O God" (Psalm 17:6). How would your life be different if you had a deeper grasp of this truth?

"From his temple he heard my voice, and my cry to him reached his ears" (Psalm 18:6). His comfort, wisdom, love, intimacy, presence, and life are available to us. Jesus tells his disciples, "I am with you always, to the end of the age" (Matthew 28:20). He is available with all his joy, with all his beauty, with all his glory. There is a divine hospitality available to us that makes God our constant friend and transforms prayer into communion.

Here is some comfort for us when we struggle with the life of prayer: our current experience of God's intimacy is not a final destination. He is available and inviting.

David the psalmist somehow had a sense of this reality even before the advent of Christ. Notice the places David draws his comfort from:

> I have set the LORD always before me;
> because he is at *my right hand*, I shall not be shaken.
>   (Psalm 16:8, emphasis added)

> In your presence there is fullness of joy;
> at *your right hand* are pleasures forevermore. (Psalm 16:11)

What sort of logic is this? Is the Lord at my right hand or am I at his? David seems to be playing games with us—but I assure you he is not. Here are the places of prayer: at the right hand of Christ, and Christ at our right hand. He is at my right hand, I am at his. One is for confidence, the other for joy.

David sensed security and confidence because the Lord was at his right hand, along with pleasures evermore and fullness of joy when he ascended to the Lord's right hand. I long for this experience, don't you? I long for a sense of safety and pleasure, confidence and joy. When was the last time you felt that?

In the fourth and fifth centuries, Augustine asked how we could be sure that this confidence is ours to experience. He wrote *De Magistro*, "The Teacher," to work it out. This book wouldn't be the last thing Augustine would write on prayer, but it created a foundation for what he would later write.

Augustine outlined the interlocking parts of prayer. (1) Prayer occurs within the "inner person." (2) Christ is located within the "inner person." (3) Christ illuminates the heart to divine reality.[3]

Augustine was working out the truth of Psalm 16 with a New Testament reality. Christ, by the Holy Spirit, relates to us like the temple. "Do you not know that *you are God's temple* and that God's Spirit dwells in you?" (1 Corinthians 3:16, emphasis added). In the Old Testament the glory of God dwelt in the temple. It was the place of prayer, instruction, and divine revelation. It's where the people met with God. Now that Christ has been sacrificed once for all, buried, and has risen again to ascend to the heavenly places, earthly temples of sacrifice are no longer needed. Now, that place is the "inner person" of those of us with faith. We are the place of glory! We are the meeting place. We are the place of prayer.

In his temple (that's us), two things occur. Christ teaches us about ourselves:

Search me, O God, and know my heart!

Try me and know my thoughts!

And see if there be any grievous way in me,

and lead me in the way everlasting! (Psalm 139:23-24)

He also teaches our hearts about God:

I pray that the eyes of your heart may be enlightened in
order that you may know the hope to which he has called
you, the riches of his glorious inheritance in his holy people.
(Ephesians 1:18 NIV)

In other words, when a Christian comes to the inner place, he
finds a place of intimacy known fully to God; however, we are
often estranged to it. We are "confronted as a stranger in his
own country."[4]

But prayer is the way of knowledge of self and the place of
friendship with God. We come to our inner place, where God
exposes our hidden motivations and subconscious longings,
heals them, and shows us himself.

Ambrose, one of Augustine's early mentors, calls this inner
person our "chamber." This is important because Augustine and
Ambrose were concerned with some popular spiritual develop-
ments of their own day. There was a growing spiritual elitism in
the major metropolitan cities like Rome and Milan. Some
monks were dwelling in the desert or harsh atmospheres where
they would experience the presence of Christ in their chamber.
This experience became an exclusive one for monks. In other
words, prayer had become merely for the spiritually elite and
those who hid away from the normal rhythms of work and
family for prayer and devotion.

I imagine not much has changed today, fifteen hundred years later. For those of us with normal, everyday jobs and families, a prayerful life can seem impractical and reserved for the elite and devoted few. So we ask our pastors and priests to pray *for* us.

But Augustine insists that prayer is for all believers. Our "chamber in the wilderness" is *within* all who have faith. The meeting place to experience the fullness of joy and pleasures forevermore is within each of us, our inner person. Prayer is not just for the spiritually elite, for those who go away to desolate places or perform feats of piety, but for you and me.

The theological explanations are complicated, but the reality is not. We are at the right hand of Christ and he is at ours. Prayer is made available to everyone, not just the spiritually elite, because the meeting place of prayer is within us. "You have your chamber everywhere."

This is God's way of saying, "Don't make this overly complicated. The place has been provided, the important thing is to enter it." There is much to say about what we are to do when we come to prayer, but most of the work and power comes from him.

If we gather up everything I've said so far, I've made some thorny complications for us. How can God be both heavy and holy (dangerous and weighty), yet close and available? How can we be raised to his right hand for joy even while he is at our right hand for comfort? We don't have intimate and joyful relationships with hurricanes, nor can we embrace the sun—but here we are with God. Two things are in tension but necessary: God's wondrous otherness and his intimate closeness.

We must never resolve this tension by deflating one or the other. We can never maintain God's *transcendence* by dismissing his *intimacy*. We must never cling to his intimacy by discarding his holiness or domesticate God by making him less complex and palatable. He is all-holy, all-beautiful, all-joyful, and all-available.

Instead of trying to resolve the tension, we sing about it and give thanks. These complexities of God ought to provoke wonder more than problem solving. Who says there's a problem anyway? Just mysteries to enjoy along the way. That's prayer, by the way. Come for the mystery, stay for the fullness.

But we can say something about it. The experience of this heavy, holy, joyful, beautiful, relational, available God comes by way of being raised up and seated with Christ at *his right hand* into his divine experiences and by way of Christ condescending with us at *our right hand* into our earthly experiences.

That almost seems too much, doesn't it? Nothing of God's transcendence and intimacy is diluted. But slowly, from one degree of glory to the next, we are being "filled to the measure of all the fullness of God" (Ephesians 3:19 NIV). Amen. Let it be so.

CHAPTER THREE

THE INVITATION OF PRAYER

"**MOST OF THEIR VICES** are attempted short cuts to love," writes John Steinbeck in *East of Eden*, a book full of characters who crave the love of a father, a brother, a lover, a son. The experience of full and satisfying love feels elusive and out of reach for Steinbeck's characters, so they often live and make decisions out of that longing. Their reaching for love sometimes produces gentleness and faithfulness, but often it manifests in resentment, selfishness, arrogance, violence, revenge, and murder.

Most of our vices are attempted shortcuts to love. I resonate with that. Don't you? We serve others in order to feel loved and needed. We long to hear from the mouths of others, "I don't know what I'd do without you." And we fear feeling disposable. So we make every effort to avoid being disposable, and we resent others when they don't notice our efforts.

Prayer is the place where we come to be healed and to experience love freely and fully. In prayer we experience God's divine welcome and joy. We experience being known and seen. God is fully present and invites us to be fully present with him. He tells us to set aside our false versions of ourselves. Just be yourself and be loved.

The problem is that we have learned and grown into impulses of proving our worth rather than receiving it freely. And that makes prayer hard. It makes awkward and uncomfortable what ought to be intimate and joyful. Annie Dillard tells us to be careful of what we learn because that is what we will know.[1] We have learned to seek love falsely, so that is what we do. A life of prayer and spiritual depth is one of learning how to experience love truly with God and then also with others. In other words, we must unlearn so much of how we seek love and intimacy.

The Christian faith teaches us that we ought to learn how to seek love and intimacy from God in the way that Christ, the Son of God, sought love and intimacy with God the Father. The more we intellectually grasp this reality, the more we will have an *experiential* grasp of it, leading to transformation.

Consider what the apostle Paul has to say about those of us with faith:

> If then you have been raised *with Christ*, seek the things that are above, where Christ is, seated at the right hand of God. Set your minds on things that are above, not on things that are on earth. For you have died, and your life is hidden *with Christ* in God. When Christ who is your life appears, then you also will appear *with him* in glory. (Colossians 3:1-4, emphasis added)

Paul is pointing out, first, what is true of Christ: he died and was buried. When Paul says "your life is hidden with Christ," *hidden* is not just an image of being safe with Christ but more like the imagery of buried treasure. You have been buried too. But then, *he was raised* from the dead on the third day. Forty days after the resurrection, Christ ascended into heaven, glorified and beautified. And at some point, he will appear "in glory." He's coming again to finally bring full restoration and healing and exaltation to the world.

Paul is not just exalting and contemplating what is true of Christ. He also grabs us by the collar and tells us, "Look at this!" He lays bare the beauty and probes into the mystery of our world with Christ. He's not just telling us about Christ, but notice the *with* language: "raised *with* Christ," "died and hidden *with* Christ," "you will appear *with* Christ in glory." These are all things that Christ has done for us, but when we become Christians, our lives become so identified *with* Christ that what is said of Christ (died, buried, risen, exalted, and revealed in glory) is also said of us! What is true of Christ is true of us. What belongs to Christ belongs to us.

When the New Testament talks about someone becoming a Christian, it almost never uses the word *Christian*. When Paul or Jesus talks about being a Christian, he uses the language of being *in* or *with* Christ. Whatever is said of Christ is said of us. What Christ has done is applied to me. The term that ancient Christians often used for this reality was *participation*. We participate with Christ in his exalted and beloved existence.

In chapter two we thought about the place of prayer. In prayer, Christ is present with me and I am present with him. Now we are talking about the posture of prayer. Paul is showing us that when we come to Christ in prayer, we can have confidence that we are loved, cherished, and welcomed in the same way that Christ is loved, cherished, and welcomed by the Father. Our past, present, and future are now identified with Christ's past, present, and future.

When Paul says, "You have died," there are radical implications for our past. Our guilt, sin, and selfish ambitions have been nailed to the cross and buried. Our sin can still sting, but its life and authority over us has been killed. We're dead to it. If we cut the head off a python, throw its body into a pit, and then jump in with the headless snake, its muscles will still thrash and whip and might even cause great damage—but there will be a limit, and soon it will run out of life completely.

For the Christian, sin is that way. Its head has been cut off. Our guilt is paid for by Christ and is buried in the ground. Although it can whip and thrash, and residue from the past can cause relational damage and pain, the power is gone, and it will not have the last word on us. Hear that again: guilt will not have the last say.

For some of us, guilt is not the problem; shame is. What we've done is not what weighs us down; it's who we are. There's a difference between the experience of guilt and the experience of shame. Guilt keeps us up at night because we've done something wrong. Shame keeps us up at night because *we* are wrong. Shame is a sense of inadequacy. We walk into encounters with others with an overwhelming sense of having to prove ourselves, so we play-act as someone we are not. But Paul says, "You have been raised and seated with Christ. His glory is your glory. His beauty has been given to you. Who you are is hidden in Christ."

Our present reality of experiencing shame and insecurity is not the true reality. We have been raised, seated. We are daughters and sons. In Christ and before the courts of heaven we don't have to prove ourselves. We don't have to be a false version of ourselves. We can simply be ourselves and loved. When you pray, repeat that last line to yourself and believe it.

Our fears for the future, too, are healed in prayer, since what is hidden in Christ about us—that we are loved and beautified—will be revealed in glory. "When Christ who is your life appears, then you also will appear with him in glory" (Colossians 3:4). If we have Christ, the ultimate truth about us is that we have been raised, ascended, and glorified. And while we may now feel guilt or shame, that we are ugly, unlovable, and ignorable, we are actually and truly an immortal splendor in Christ—and God already looks at us that way. There will come a day when who we truly are in Christ will be made clear, and we'll finally recognize it. Then we will say to each other, "Now I know who you truly are."

We fear many things about the future. We fear loss, loneliness, death—or what's just around the corner. But in Christ, what we fear will not have the last word.

On the cross Christ's body was torn and people looked away. But now, in glory, he has been beautified, and no one can stop looking. In his suffering Christ was humiliated, forsaken, and forgotten. Now, in heaven, he is exalted and fully loved. He was scorned but now is cherished; whipped but now kissed; beaten but now embraced. He was forgotten but now is remembered forever. What is true of Christ is true of us, and someday we will experience that reality in full. That is our future. Let that future inform your fears.

According to the New Testament a Christian is someone who is in Christ, and Christians increasingly understand themselves —their past, their present, and their future—in Christ. The determining factor in my life is not my past, present, and future, but Christ's past, present, and future. In Christ our guilt, shame, and fears are all healed. We have all the resources in Christ to increasingly sense that healing in prayer.

Eugene Peterson describes a life that does not live out this truth.

> We perform in order to get God's approval . . . religious or moral activity designed to save our own skin. Good behavior that is performed because someone else is looking or because God is looking. It is a life by performance, show, achievement. And of course it imprisons us because someone is always looking. It makes us into calculating people, not free people. Calculating what my actions will produce in others. What will they think of me? Do I fit into what others expect? How will God reward us? What penalties will be avoided? This is not freedom. Calculating your actions is not freedom. Freedom is coming into every moment, every situation, every room with the reality of already being loved, accepted, and approved.[2]

Living without grasping who we are and what we in Christ puts us into a calculating existence.

Inspector Gamache, the main character in Louise Penny's crime mystery novel *Still Life* is an older, seasoned detective. Near the middle of the story, there is an emotional moment when Gamache takes a risk and ends up suspended from his position. His badge and gun are taken away. Without these, he is vulnerable and afraid. The voices of his insecure youth come back, saying that his badge is what made him *somebody*. With it, he has meaning and importance. Without it, he's nobody.

Gamache remembers an old analogy a mentor once shared with him that life was like living in a long house.

> We enter as babies on one end, and exited when our time came. And in between we moved through this one great long room. Everyone we ever met and every thought and action live in that room with us. Until we made peace with the less agreeable parts of our past they'd continue to heckle us from way down the long house. And sometimes the really loud obnoxious ones told us what to do, directing our actions even years later.[3]

Gamache wasn't sure he agreed with that analogy until the moment he'd had to place his badge on his supervisor's desk. The insecure young man was revived and whispered, "You're nothing without it. What will people think? You will be forgotten and a nobody." Realizing how inappropriate the reaction was didn't banish the fearful young man from the long house. He wondered, *Is that whispering voice still in charge?*

A calculating existence means we live our lives making decisions, walking into every room and every meeting with a whispering voice: *You're nothing without this! What will people think of me? You cannot let them truly see you. You are forgettable.* That voice is always in charge.

But a life that grasps who we are in Christ hears another voice whispering in our ear, "Well done, good and faithful servant." "You are my beloved child, in whom I'm well pleased." "I love you." "Enter into my joy. You've got nothing to prove. You're free." That voice is in charge because we know in our heart of hearts that what is true of Christ is true of us.

The determining factor in our lives is not our past, present, and future, but Christ's past, present, and future. That is what it means to mature in Christ: to learn to hear the voice of Christ more than any other.

"Love takes off the masks that we fear we cannot live without and know we cannot live within," says James Baldwin.[4] Coming to prayer in Christ gives us the divine experience that heals us and takes off our masks.

I once talked with an older friend about prayer when I was going through a season of pain and depression. My insecurities were flaring up and I needed direction. My friend encouraged me to read the Bible and then meditate on the Scriptures as if they were God's words to me at that moment. That small practice refreshed my prayers.

I still practice this regularly, but I've developed it and made it more personal. Instead of imagining God speaking to me in general, I mediate on the passage as if God the Father is speaking, then God the Son, then God the Spirit. If I read Deuteronomy 31:8, "The LORD himself goes before you and will be with you; he will never leave you nor forsake you. Do not be afraid; do not be discouraged" (NIV), I ask myself, how might the Father speak that same truth to me in order to assure me of his fatherly love? How might the Son, my brother, advocate, and friend, speak that truth to me? What might the Spirit, the counselor, convicter, and comforter say?

THE FATHER

Imagine how God the Father would communicate Deuteronomy 31:8 to you. You come to him like the prodigal son, returning home to his father's love. The prodigal has been wandering from home, tired, guilty, and poor, and now he wants to return home. Have you ever returned to prayer feeling like that? The prodigal assumes he can't merely return as a son. He's squandered his inheritance. So he plans to come back as a servant. It's what he deserves. He has an entire speech ready for his father.

But when the father sees his son returning home, he embraces him with joy. The father interrupts his son's speech to call for a robe, a ring for his finger, and a fattened calf to be slaughtered. His son is home (Luke 15:11-32)!

When we come back to prayer from our wanderings, our sin, our failures, we come with speeches, with explanations, with promises: "I'll serve you better." "I'll make it up to you." And the Father interrupts us with kisses on our neck and a feast for the welcome. He says, "Do not be afraid and do not be discouraged. I will never leave you nor forsake you."

We are the forsaking sons and daughters, but he is the running, welcoming, embracing, and feasting Father. Come to prayer with repentance and neediness, not speeches.

THE SON

The Son shows us everything that's his and reminds us that it's ours too. He whispers the words of Deuteronomy 31:8 to us. "Why are you discouraged? I am the Lord who goes before you." He is, isn't he? He has gone before us. He went before us to the cross, to the grave, and to the heavens, making a way for us. "I go and prepare a place for you," he reminds us in John 14:3.

But in preparing a place for us, Christ has not left us. In God's mystery Christ has gone before us, but he is still with us.

Augustine tells us that Christ is closer to us than we are to our-selves. Why should we be afraid? He knows us more deeply than we know ourselves, and he has not left us once.

Imagine all that Christ can whisper to us for comfort. What might a rescuer say to the imprisoned? What might an heir say to his fellow heir who feels impoverished? What might the resurrected say to those who fear death? What might the one who experienced homelessness say to us when we lust for larger homes? What might the One tempted by Satan in the wil-derness say to the tempted? What might the One whose best friends couldn't stay up and pray for him in the darkest of nights say to those of us who feel alone in our struggles? What might the One who was betrayed say to us when we feel blindsided? What might the One who prayed with bloody sweat in the garden say to us when we are anxious? What might the One who cried out, "My God, my God why have you forsaken me?" say to us when we feel abandoned, forsaken, and forgotten?

Jesus says to us,

- I will be with you. (Matthew 28:20)

- I will never leave you nor forsake you. (Hebrews 13:5)

- I am praying for you. (1 John 2:1)

- I will come back for you. (John 14:3)

- I leave you a Comforter. (John 14:16)

- Come to me for rest. (Matthew 11:28-30)

- Take heart, I have overcome the world. (John 16:33)

- You will be with me in paradise. (Luke 23:43)

- You are my friend. (John 15:15)

- I am not ashamed to call you brother and sister. (Hebrews 2:11)

THE SPIRIT

The Spirit points us to all the riches. He tells us of all the glory of Christ and reminds us that we are heirs with Jesus. He whispers words of comfort, conviction, and courage. If we're listening, the Spirit helps us think straight. He points beyond this world to healing, hope, and joy. He teaches us how to pray, and when we don't have words, he groans for us (Romans 8:23).

The believer listening for the Spirit, Balthasar teaches us, "catches fire and radiates with heightened presence" by the intense heat of the Spirit.[5] The Spirit is "more interior to us than we are to ourselves."[6] There is no better person to show us our true self and show us how to take off our masks, transforming us into our true self in Christ. The Spirit is the great Comforter, Counselor, and Friend. Of course, he has something to say to us. "Do not fear," he says, reminding us of all the promises of the Father and all the accomplishments of Christ (from Deuteronomy 31). "If God is for us, who can be against us?" (Romans 8:31). If the Father did not spare his own Son, the Spirit reasons, but gave him up for us all, why would he not give us everything we need and more (Romans 8:32)? Why be afraid?

God, who is beyond, with, and within, loves us freely and fully. Prayer is coming to receive that love, as the prodigal received the father's feast.

CHAPTER FOUR

OUTGROWING THE
REACTIONARY HEART

I MINISTER IN A BUSY AND VIBRANT CITY. Things happen fast and decisions are made rapidly. "Think on your feet," we say. Restaurants on my block close almost as quickly as they open. People move, jobs change, economies shift, and trends emerge—all of it at full speed. Are you keeping up? We're tempted to live in this environment merely as people reacting to changing stimuli.

Living in a big, bustling environment like New York quickly exposes that we live *reactionary* lives. But this is more likely true of all of us, whether we live in city centers, suburban cul-de-sacs, or off rural highways. I am not talking about temperament. It's not just an easygoing disposition versus someone around whom we have to walk on pins and needles. A *reactionary* life acts in response to what happens rather than out of our inner lives. We often do not know how to handle what the world throws at us. We simply react. When others hurt us, we react with anger, bitterness, and resentment, moving us to hurt back or pass the pain down the line to someone else. When we lose our job, we respond with anxiety and have quick, spastic reactions. Or when we are offered more money, we take it without knowing how to count other costs. This isn't a big-city problem, it's a human one.

Reactionary lives lead to empty and confused hearts, making us prisoners to a changing world. It's impossible to be truly loving with a reactionary spiritual life. With a reactionary heart, joy depends on circumstantial ease or success rather than being sustained through all the spheres of life. Self-control is only possible when we are in control of our surroundings.

Christian maturity, says Henri Nouwen, calls us to a gradual movement from "an anxious reaction to a loving response," where we "can listen to the events of the hour, the day, and the year and slowly 'formulate,' give form to, a response that is really our own."[1] Moving beyond a reactionary spiritual life helps us make decisions and respond in ways that are more courageous than fearful, more free than enslaved.

A life of prayer and stillness with God is the place reactionary hearts go to die and be raised as something deeper. We must be alert to the formation of our *spirit* and our *soul*.

There's a long and complex dialogue about the difference between our spirit and soul (or body, spirit, and soul) that we don't have space to parse here. But the Bible often uses the language of *soul* and *spirit* synonymously, yet at other times it refers to them as two different realities. A soul and spirit are two concepts the Bible uses to help us climb for the mountain tops of life and to get us through valleys of shadows.

David Benner explains how the language of spirit and soul is used in Scripture through the lens of human longing and experience.[2] Our spirit is what makes us alive to the world. It is what energizes and makes us alert to our hopes; what keeps us moving toward goals and ambitions. When Jesus died, he "yielded up his *spirit*" (Matthew 27:50, emphasis added); Paul commands us to be "fervent in *spirit*" (Romans 12:11, emphasis added); when we are brokenhearted, we are "crushed in *spirit*" (Psalm 34:18, emphasis added); a "willing *spirit*" comes from the joy of salvation (Psalm 51:12, emphasis added); our spirits "faint within us" when troubles come (Psalm 142:3).

Our spirit helps us imagine a future and puts meaning into everything we do. It ignites and moves us, makes us dream big dreams and expect big things. A healthy and robust spirit puts fire in our bellies and makes us run. A crushed spirit doesn't want to get out of bed. It has lost hope and can't see around the corner.

The soul contains and directs our passions. "If the spirit is the fire in our bellies," says Benner, "we immediately see the need for something that can help us contain this fire, sometimes even cool it down. We need a womb of safety and containment."[3] An enriched soul puts depth to our dreaming and helps us "bear what is intolerable in the world."[4] There is always plenty of danger, pain, and heartache, and the soul allows us to hold all the unanswered prayer, all the betrayal, all the loss, and not be overwhelmed.

An enriched spirit is needed because God has made us in his image. We are called to be fruitful and creative in this world.

We need to imagine great and hopeful things for our life and others' lives. We need enriched souls to put dignity in ordinary, mundane work. "While the soul makes its home in the deep, shaded valley, the spirit seeks a place in the bright light on the mountaintop."[5] We need souls to make sense of suffering, pain, and abandonment.

"Do not be slothful in zeal," Paul says, "be fervent in spirit, serve the Lord" (Romans 12:11). That's the fire in the belly. *Fervent* literally means "aglow." Serving the Lord with zeal and a glowing spirit.

In the next verse, Paul writes, "Rejoice in hope, be patient in tribulations, be constant in prayer" (v. 12). We can only rejoice in hope if what we're hoping for isn't here yet. We need an enriched spirit to serve the Lord with zeal in this world, and we need a soul to be patient when our world falls apart, still praying, still hoping, even if it's with a pounding fist.

With an enriched soul and spirit, we aren't afraid to hope for great and wonderful things, and we aren't resentful when things don't happen the way we planned. Fear of hoping too much and resistance to dreaming are the fruits of a crushed spirit and a diminished soul. An enriched spirit points us to transcendence, and an enriched soul holds us together when we experience what we would never choose.

This vision of the spiritual life forms us to receive the world as it truly is, not some fabrication of what we would hope it to be. We begin to respond with joy and gratitude in all things. Not suddenly, not even quickly, but slowly and surely. Here the reactionary life dies. We begin to relearn impulses to both mountaintop joys and deep valley sorrows. "The righteous . . . is not afraid of bad news" (Psalm 112:6-7). We need a heightened spirit and depth of soul for that kind of courage. The psalmist is not describing someone who never takes risks or imagines great things so that he may never be disappointed! He's describing someone ambitiously dreaming for the skies and not afraid when it crashes to the ground.

But this life isn't something we merely agree to and then live. No, it's a life we *grow* into. The person not afraid of bad news likely has a spirit and soul two or three times larger than ours. We will need to find ways of growing.

A Christian who wants to grow out of a reactionary life and into an enriched soul and spirit must learn to pray the psalms. Does that surprise you? The psalms teach us how to encounter the world and live as fully human in it, as God intended. The psalms provide words to say to our enemies, to God, and to ourselves.

Take, for instance, Psalm 31. David is in trouble. He's in danger of being put to shame (v. 1). His enemies have set a trap for him (v. 4). His life is full of sorrow and grief (vv. 9-10). He has been forgotten (v. 12), and death seems imminent (v. 13). Yet he's a man full of confidence! "I will rejoice and be glad in your steadfast love!" (v. 7). "You have set my feet in a broad place" (v. 8). "Oh, how abundant is your goodness" (v. 19), he sings, "for he has wondrously shown his steadfast love to me" (v. 21). "Be strong," he exhorts his readers, "and let your heart take courage!" (v. 24).

For David there is a tension of distress and confidence that's otherworldly. He's describing two normal experiences of life: one that is full of trouble, anger, fear, and anxiety, and another that is full of life, as if the wind of the world is at his back, all his prayers seem answered, and God seems present. It's almost as if this psalm is written by two different people or in two different seasons of life. It's a vision of life in which the gap between those two normal human experiences is nonexistent, where despite the real distress, there's strange confidence and joy.

David has done this before, in Psalm 23. As "I walk through the valley of the shadow of death, I will fear no evil. . . . You prepare a table before me in the presence of my enemies" (vv. 4-5). That's a striking image. He's feeling two experiences. One is the pressure and distress of his enemies closing in. The other is the experience of God's presence, which he describes like a table of feasting being prepared for him. A feast to enjoy in the midst of his encroaching enemies. That's remarkable.

Psalms 31 and 23 are a kind of microcosm of the experience of praying the psalms. They teach us how to experience the world as it comes to us through prayer. In some ways the psalms teach us what it means to experience the world with faith—real, earthy, feet-to-the-ground faith. And the evidence of our faith in moments of mountaintop joy or valley-floor despair is what we do with the real emotions that come—because they do come. To experience fear, anger, despair, depression, or anxiety isn't a lack of faith. Our faith is evident in what we do with these emotions. David's expression of faith in these psalms is evidence that he is not an escapist. He does not avoid his emotions. He's not sweeping them under the rug or hiding. He is clearly exposing his fears to God, who already sees and knows. David knows that he will never be healed if he doesn't bring his emotions, his fears, and his anger into God's presence.

Prayer must include some healthy exploration of our emotional life. This is not navel-gazing but holding still enough to

see ourselves clearly. For many of us this means we do not escape
to our phones, our email, or our social media feeds when emotions prove overwhelming. We hold on and look in. It's not easy.

"Cast your anxieties on him," Peter tells us (1 Peter 5:7). But
we can only do that if we know our anxieties. We sometimes
think people who examine their emotions are emotionally un-
healthy. But it's the people who choose to escape from them who
are unstable. We examine our fears, then pray them. We take a
good look at our anger and call on God to heal us from it.

God doesn't want us with happy words and heavy hearts.
The psalmists teach us to speak truthfully. Take Psalm 88 as an
example. Reading this psalm can make the pious among us
blush. It's a psalm of complaint. It's uncomfortable reading.
The psalmist is almost too honest; we might feel the need to
say, "Don't talk that way." If our children prayed this way, we'd
likely hush them. "Don't talk that way to God!" Yet here it is
in the psalms.

Psalm 88 is a lament in the form of complaint—not a complaint against his enemies but against God. Here's what he's
experiencing: *Judgment*—"You [the LORD] have put me in the
depths of the pit, in the regions dark and deep" (v. 6), "Your
wrath lies heavy upon me" (v. 7), "your dreadful assaults destroy
me" (v. 16). "O LORD, why do you cast my soul away? Why do
you hide your face from me?" (v. 14). *Unanswered prayer*—"I cry
out day and night before you" (v. 1), but God never answers. He
begins his day with prayer and ends his day with crying out to God,
yet the Lord hides "[his] face from me" (v. 14). *Abandonment*
—"You have caused my companions to shun me; you have made
me a horror to them" (v. 8). "You have caused my beloved and my

friend to shun me; my companions have become darkness" (v. 18). A better translation of verse 18 is "darkness has become my closest friend." Darkness, claims the psalmist, is a closer friend than you, Lord.

This is startling language. Are we allowed to talk to God this way? You almost want to encourage the man to go on a walk, take a few deep breaths, and then come back to prayer. But no, here it is. Now, if this is God's Word, *why did God allow this psalm in?* Why didn't he edit it out? If Psalms is God's hymnal and praise book, why did he allow a song that is so full of complaint against him? Isn't that remarkable?

But God is not so insecure and unsure of himself that he can't take our criticism. God not only allows these words, he is ultimately the author of them. The wondrous thing about Psalm 88 is that in it the Lord gives his people words to say when we're numb with pain. This is a prayer for the troubled. Derek Kidner says, "The very presence of this psalm in the Bible shows us that God hasn't abandoned those who are full of trouble and despair, but that he is still with them. He wrote this psalm because he knows how men speak when they are desperate."[6] Psalm 88 is God's way of giving us words when we don't have any or maybe when we are fearful to express what we are thinking.

Athanasius said it best, "Most Scriptures speak to us; the Psalms speak for us."[7]

To pray along with the angry, confused, and desperate psalms is to trust that God knows what to do with our emotions. It is to put on the emotional depth of the psalms. These psalms enlarge our hearts and deepen our experience of the world, ourselves, and God. "For centuries," Eugene Peterson writes, "from the beginning, if Christians wanted to learn how to pray, they would open their Bibles to the Psalms and pray them; faithfully and for a lifetime. That's how most Christians for most of the Christian centuries have matured in prayer."[8]

This formation in prayer is slow work. I remember talking with a graduate student about prayer. He was a new Christian. He didn't know how to pray but was eager to learn. I told him prayer doesn't come once we learn a technique or a few steps; it comes like a runner's endurance. Prayer is like a muscle. People who have learned to pray and have had a simple, daily but faithful prayer life, whether for ten years or for fifty, will tell you it's like marathon running. You run with growing freedom and joy the more you do it.

His confidence was high and he half ignored my remark. The next time we met, he came with the confession that he didn't take my advice seriously about prayer being like a muscle because he had the ability to study for several hours at a time and had remarkable focus. Prayer seemed like something he could easily handle. But he confessed that prayer was hard. He assumed he was using the same mechanism to pray that he was using to study.

Certainly, there is an intellectual side to prayer, and if you have a short attention span, prayer will be a deeper and different struggle. But something of the soul is used in prayer and communion that doesn't get exercised in intellectual endeavors. For many of us modern people, it doesn't get stirred much during our lives. Even though as Christians we recognize our need to pray (and in fact our love and desire compels us to), we often feel like a wet match trying to strike a flame.

Imagine someone who had spent his twenties living entirely for himself. He left home without much regard for his family, went after relationships as a means for pleasure rather than for friendship or companionship, and used his coworkers as rungs on a ladder. Suddenly, he falls in love. He *feels* as if he can sacrifice anything for this person.

But love and sacrifice don't happen on a whim. People fall in love, but they don't fall into sacrificial love. That takes humility and work. The person who spends their life being self-indulgent in relationships will find it impossible to be sacrificial in a snap.

So it is with prayer. There's an inner part of us that's exercised and strengthened, stretched and shaped when we pray. For many of us that part lies dormant for long seasons of our lives. Listening is hard; knowing how to listen in prayer is harder. We don't know how to be silent. The clutter and voices of everyday life fill the void quickly. Fears and shame strangle our solitude. I once wrote a prayer in my journal: "Father, I wish my communion with you would distract me from my worries rather than my worries distracting me from you." I wonder if you resonate with that prayer.

Much of what God is doing in us is slow, quiet work. It isn't normally radical progress. Often when we ask for God's help or God's presence, we overlook his answer because we don't know how to see. Prayer exposes what God is doing. It shapes us into people who know how to be patient with his work. Prayer keeps us in step with him.

Jesus' first miracle was to turn water into wine at a wedding where there was a goof in the wedding planning. This was his first "sign"—his calling card—and no one knew he performed the miracle except "the servants who had drawn the water knew" (John 2:9). Isn't it interesting that the next big exposé comes in John 4, where the first person that Jesus shows his identity as the Messiah to was a moral outcast, the Samaritan woman?

The first sign and first disclosure of Jesus' identity was to forgettable servants and a needy sinner. Throughout the Gospels we find Jesus resisting the powerful and the pompous and going to the outcast and the humble. Wasn't it the "teacher of Israel," Nicodemus, who missed what Jesus was doing, even though he was looking? If we want to see and experience what God does in us and around us, which is quiet and subtle, we must make ourselves low. Prayer is the regular practice of lowering ourselves to better views of his work.

It's a strange irony that prayer is the strengthening of an inner muscle that does nothing more than boast in weakness. Prayer gives us ears to hear, knowing we do not listen well, and eyes to see, knowing we are blind to much of what we ought to see. But along the way God transforms our anxious reactions into loving responses, and our fearful hearts into hearts that are not afraid of bad news.

CHAPTER FIVE

PAIN AND PRAYER

IN 1985, HENRI NOUWEN left his position at Harvard Divinity School in Boston to serve at L'Arche in Trosly, France, a ministry to the mentally disabled. He gave up the prestige of an Ivy League school for a vocation that was "forgotten and passed over."[1] The mentally disabled are often forgotten, and they often don't have the capacity to be grateful for the care they receive.[2]

Within the first several months of Nouwen's new life, a close friend from Boston was traveling to Paris and had promised to spend time with him in Trosly. But his friend returned to Boston without even a note or call of explanation. The pain of rejection stung Nouwen. For the first time he felt the forgottenness of his new vocation, but he had not expected it from a friend.

"I now wonder what to do with this experience," he wrote in his journal. Whenever the pain of rejection arose again, he would remind himself, "If you really want to be less visible, less known, try to use this event to become more forgotten, more passed over; be grateful for the occasion. Trust that hiddenness will give you new eyes to see yourself, your world, and your God. People cannot give you new eyes; only the one who loves you without limits."[3] One of the reasons he had moved to minister to the mentally disabled was to still the deep desire of his heart to be known or applauded for his work. He had enjoyed the attention he had received in his prestigious Ivy League position. Now he was seeking a more hidden life in work that was just as important but rarely noticed. And here was a moment, an occasion of being forgotten, when he could practice what this truly meant.

Nouwen prayed for help not to be bitter and angry at his friend. As he reflected, he realized that it would take some time to understand and fully forgive. "Meanwhile," he says, "I am trying to keep a sense of humor and write a few notes to people who are always close to thinking that I am rejecting them."

In Nouwen's short journal entry we find a narrative of how he responded to the feelings of rejection. First, he reflected on what to do with these feelings. He was confused and hurt, but nevertheless honest about his emotions. He didn't stuff them down. Second, he brought his emotions and pain to God, asking for help in what he knew he should do—that is, forgive and not be bitter—and worked to remind himself of what he knew to be true about his vocation and standing in the world. Third, he recognized his human weakness in overcoming the pain with forgiveness and asked God for help. Finally, the occasion helped him become aware of the ways he had caused others to feel rejected by him. He committed to a more loving correspondence with others.

Something that Nouwen does not mention, but which was obvious to me, was the *time* and *space* he gave for reflection, lament, and self-correction. The circumstance provoked pain and feelings of rejection. Nouwen didn't squash the feelings, nor did he quickly deem them illegitimate. Instead, he brought his emotions to the Lord intentionally and methodically, giving him time to heal and correct.

I made a note in the margins of Nouwen's journal entry, "Where do I make time for this kind of reflection?" Too often I move on quickly when others cause me pain. I'm not honest about the inner bitterness and anger stewing. I put a pillow over it so that no one sees and hope that maybe it'll be forgotten. But at some point it does come out. Eventually, it will find its way out, but it won't be a prayer or lament. Instead, it will be malice and suffering either in me or toward my neighbor.

Is giving this much thought to our pain indulgent? Just move on, right?

What human experience and the book of Psalms show us over and over again is that forgiveness and healing are difficult and costly. We know we should forgive, but our hearts don't run as fast as our intellects because they carry heavier baggage. It requires more time and patience, more care and reflection. The psalms teach us we have little control over our emotions. The little power we have is where we take them.

This process does not make Nouwen a more self-indulgent sulker. Instead, he learns to consider how others might feel wounded by him and makes some corrections in his own life. This, in a nutshell, is soul care.

The difficult thing about soul care is that it's not very practical, at least in the way we'd like it to be. It doesn't produce immediate fruit, and the transformation is slow. But when we ignore it, hardness grows and our inner life suffers and shrivels.

This is the lesson of prayer during seasons of pain: the fruit of healing and restoration takes time. It won't come any other way. We have little patience for this sort of waiting. In our consumerist age, we are used to the engine of efficiency: if the product doesn't come fast or on our terms, then we turn to something else. But in prayer we aren't consumers, we're participants. Healing doesn't come fast, and it's rarely on our terms.

Months later, Nouwen wrote in his journal:

> It is hard for me to forgive someone who has really offended me, especially when it happens more than once. I begin to doubt the sincerity of the one who asks forgiveness for a second, third, or fourth time. But God does not keep count. God just waits for our return, without resentment or desire for revenge. God wants us home. . . . Maybe the reason it seems hard for me to forgive others is that I do not fully believe that I am a forgiven person. If I could fully accept the truth that I am forgiven and do not have to live in guilt or shame, I would really be free. My freedom would allow me to forgive others seventy times seven times.[4]

It is a comfort to know we can bring our pain to prayer. But what about when prayer brings pain to us? Hans Urs von

Balthasar, who wrote much on prayer, said, "As long as we stand under the law of sin, prayer will always have a painful side to it."[5] Does that surprise you? It isn't merely that prayer is a discipline and discipline is painful. Prayer's pain is more severe.

Prayer is the business of conquering territory within us—territory we think is ours but that God claims for himself. Prayer is the intentional act of vulnerability to God's claim on our lives.

This picture of prayer opposes the popular view, which sees prayer as self-expression. The psalms *do* invite honest expression, loud cries, accusations (against God even), horror, lament, fear, and so on. God invites us in to express our longings and needs. But prayer is communion, and the relationship goes two ways. Prayer is not only God merely responding to our self-expression and needs; it is also our response to God and his Word. God invites us to come freely, but we should expect to be changed.

Throughout Christian history, the practice of prayer has mainly been a response to God's Word, to what he has said about himself and what he has said about us. We read and contemplate God's Word, placing our hearts and imaginations in the words and stories. We do this in his presence, asking that he will help us see and notice what he has for us.

If you read the Bible, you will see that God's Word is often compared to a sword, and his presence to fire. These images teach us that the Word of God and his presence are not always comfortable. Swords pierce deep and cut away; fire burns and purifies.

If we come to the Bible and read it on its own terms, it will divide our hearts, separating us from our lusts and false loves. If we come to commune with God in his presence, we must be prepared for pain. He shows us where our hearts are in conflict with his heart, and he will burn away the chaff and purify us.

In his book *A Secular Age*, Charles Taylor writes that we live in the "age of authenticity."[6] It's an authenticity that boasts of the "weakness" or "messiness" of life. Leaders can gain a following by showing the "raw" elements of their life, the imperfections, the "beauty in the chaos." Christians, too, have inherited this way of talking about weakness and confession, though it is alien to the New Testament. These are confessions of imperfections on our terms. It is a laissez-faire spirituality that boasts of weakness but is safe from criticism and reproof. This sort of authenticity seeks to confess in order to be merely received. Christianity is quite different. Christianity also boasts of weakness (see the apostle Paul), but makes the self vulnerable to change and transformation.

The authentic self says, "This is me; you must accept me as I am." The vulnerable self says, "This is me; take me and transform me." The vulnerable self comes not merely in confession but in repentance. It looks not for power and affirmation but for divine help and deliverance.

Let's confess this together: We are not good at this. We have learned to resist vulnerability, so we experience something less than transformation and joy in prayer. Where does this resistance come from?

In 1944, Jean-Paul Sartre wrote in his famous play *No Exit* that "Hell is other people." Most people use the line as a complaint that other people are miserable and we'd rather be alone. But in fact, Sartre is referring to the fear of being *known* by other people. And not just known but known all the way down. He's referring to the terror that if they really knew us—our thoughts, our motives, our desires—no one would love us. They would be repelled. Hell is other people seeing you for who you truly are. It's the problem, says Sartre, of the "look of the Other." And Sartre suggests we will never be free of this hell until we are completely alone and unknown.[7]

Beginning with Adam and Eve, the Old Testament often uses the language of "walking before God." It's a Hebrew idiom that means being fully known, fully vulnerable, open, and loved—no shame, no hiding, and no judgment. In Genesis 2:25 we read that Adam and Eve were "both naked and were not ashamed." This doesn't merely mean they were unashamed of their bodies. It means they weren't afraid to be known. They could trust the gaze of the other—that they could be seen all the way through and be loved completely. They were truly at home.

What Sartre describes in his play is the reality of the world—a curse—while the beginning of Genesis describes a blessing. If we want to escape the judgment of others, argues Sartre, we need to be less vulnerable. Sartre insists that if we're being honest, we'll admit that this *hell-is-other-people* dynamic is the way the world is and how we often experience it. We are living under a curse. We often sense physical, emotional, personal, and relational homelessness. To be vulnerable to someone's gaze feels like judgment. And if hell is other people, then who is God?

What were those first few moments in Genesis like when the blessing was lost and the curse was felt? Suddenly the gaze of Adam felt more like an appraisal than love. *Hell is other people,* Eve must have thought, *so I must cover myself lest he see me.* And if the gaze of Adam felt like hell, what did the gaze of God feel like? What did she feel as she was searching for branches and leaves to cover her naked body and suddenly sensed the Lord walking through the Garden in the cool of the day? "Who told you that you were naked?" (Genesis 3:11).

I imagine Eve aching for the times when she didn't know what it meant to be naked. But here they were, covered and hiding, wondering and fearful of what the other was thinking. Somehow these strewn-together leaves and branches were not doing the job. Something deeper than their naked bodies was being exposed, and something greater than leaves would be needed.

The Lord "made for Adam and for his wife garments of skins and clothed them" (Genesis 3:21). Garments of skin. In other words, something, for the first time in history, had to die for sin. For the first time, blood had to be shed and a life was poured out that we might be clothed and our shame covered. As the story continues through Genesis and the rest of human history, we see that the skins were not adequate covering—but they did point to a life, and blood, that would be sufficient.

We find ourselves in the place of Adam and Eve, exposed and scrambling for cover. We feel seen and judged. If hell is other people, then who is God? Who can pray at a time like this?

Here we are again back to the impossibility of prayer. But there is good news. In Christ, the Lord provides new robes of righteousness, garments that invite us to approach God as if we were as beautiful, heroic, and faithful as Jesus. Christ provides a way to pray prayers like Psalm 139, where the psalmist cries, "Search me, O God, and know my heart!" (v. 23).

Now let's stop right there. That is a terrifying request to make of a being who is able to see you right down to the bottom. "Try me and know my thoughts."

Try me. Take my thoughts and don't just look at the surface of things but put them under the microscope and see what's behind and underneath, "See if there be any grievous way in me" (v. 24). No, don't! "See if there be any grievous way in me, and lead me in the way everlasting." I love that last part. Lead me in the way everlasting. It means that God's seeing me and knowing me isn't the last word before judgment or abandonment. God's searching feels like fire, and his leading feels like the thrust of a sword. But he heals me. He leads me in the way everlasting.

Here is the way we modern, authentic people can grow in vulnerability: we can learn to trust his searching and looking. It isn't easy or comfortable. We cannot do it alone. We will need other brothers and sisters, pastors and saints along the way reminding us not to hide behind false clothes and coverings.

He sees us all the way to the bottom but loves us to the skies. Prayer is the regular experience of being fully known and fully loved.

One lesson we have to learn to grow in prayer is what to do after we sin. I don't just mean small sins (as if there are such things) but the deep and disturbing ones. The ones that shock and disturb us. The ones we hope no one knows about and pretend God doesn't much notice. Or the sins we *were* caught in and that God has certainly registered as an offense. Here's a question for us to consider in our life of prayer: What do we do in response to sin?

The longer I live as a Christian the more I'm beginning to realize that a mark of Christian maturity is not merely the ability to resist sin but how we respond to our sin. The human impulse is to hide and cover, like Adam and Eve. "Who told you you were naked?" God asks us.

When people's dark corners are exposed to others and God, I often see, as a pastor, their desire to hide, to run. I see this in myself. Maybe we'll mask it in humble or religious lingo: "I can't come to church after this past week; I would feel like a hypocrite singing hymns right now." "I can't pray; I just feel too ashamed." Or maybe we don't vocalize anything. We just feel too ashamed to come to God in prayer and worship, so we don't. Consider what we're actually saying, "I need to put some space between me and my sin."

And so time goes by. We're feeling better. We feel less ashamed and go to God in prayer, participate in corporate worship, and take the Lord's Supper.

But what has happened? We feel less ashamed because we're now more emotionally distant from our sin. Maybe we've had fewer moral failures since then. But what really covers our sin isn't enough time but a sufficient sacrifice.

Adam and Eve taught us to hide and wait until we feel better about ourselves before we come in prayer. But we have a better hope than a sewn-together self-confidence. We have Christ as our High Priest. Our shame has already been covered, our sin has already been clothed with the blood and righteousness of Christ. Who told you you were naked?

When we sin, our only hope is to come to Christ. Our only confidence is to come trusting in his forgiveness and love. Our only assurance is that he loves us and will not leave us unchanged if we come to him in prayer.

So come with all your sins. Come vulnerable to his sword and fire.

Coming to God vulnerably in prayer takes a good bit of humility, and humility doesn't come easy to any of us. Humility often comes through humiliation. I wish it were different, but it's the truth. We learn humility through humiliating failure, and we humans provide ample opportunity for such lessons.

But for Christians there's a gift on the other side of humiliation. As much as I wish humility could just come through focused prayer (though it certainly won't come without it), the Lord works in us through the fire of circumstances, not just through a still, small voice.

Dan Allender writes,

> No one is humble by nature. . . . Humility comes from humiliation, not from the choice to be self-effacing or a strong urge to give others the credit.
>
> Humility that has not come from suffering due to one's own arrogance is either a pragmatic strategy to get along with others or a natural predilection that seems to befit only a few rare individuals. For most, humility comes only by wounds suffered from foolish falls.[8]

Nouwen writes that he was struggling to accomplish all that he wanted in the hours provided in the day. He wrote that he longed for God "to slow that sun down!" "But," he wrote, "it keeps going as always, round and round and round. No faster, no slower. Twenty-four hours each day." And then Nouwen received word that one of the articles he had submitted for publication—one of the best, he thought—had been rejected. The rejection letter said the article "is not up to the standard that we are used to from Henri Nouwen." "Well," he reflects, "that might slow *me* down instead of the sun."

"Life is humbling," he wrote. "Very, very humbling. I have to let it be that way. Somebody said today, 'We need a lot of humiliation for a little bit of humility.'" [9]

Unfortunately, that's true. It's a mercy, but a severe one. I find it surprising. I don't think I've normally considered the road of humiliation as one that God primarily uses for humility. Sure, suffering and loss seem like obvious means for humility, but while humiliation is a form of suffering, I don't think I've usually considered it this way. We often talk about suffering in the form of loss—loss of health, loss of a job, loss of loved ones. But we don't talk about humiliation. It could be because other forms of suffering can be seen as noble. Going through chronic pain or a job loss is extremely difficult, but suffered in the right way it's honorable. We esteem those who suffer, especially those who go through it with a buoyant trust in God. But humiliation is just humiliating. It takes away the self-worth we've stored up. It strips us. It's painful. So why wouldn't God use it?

We are resistant to humiliation, yet we needn't be. There's a communion that comes with it, if we have the eyes to see. There's a nearness to God that, at first, may feel like death but is really working to get the death out of us.

Humiliation teaches us where we have overextended our competencies and thought too highly of ourselves. It teaches us that we are needy. Time and emotional distance from our sins cannot make us morally competent before God; only his blood can do that. We must not wait until we feel better about ourselves before we come to God; that's just pride masked by self-loathing. Coming quickly to God in repentance is a sign of humility, of putting all our trust in the blood of Christ, knowing that we have no worthiness in ourselves. Sometimes a good bit of humiliation is just the thing to teach us to embody this vulnerability with God.

In our humiliation we can sense Christ's humiliation for us. There's a mystery in humility that brings us near the cross, where we share in his sufferings. As Nouwen says, "A pruned vine does not look beautiful, but during harvest time it produces much fruit."[10]

CHAPTER SIX

WAITING AND PRAYER

"'IT'S GONE!' SIGHED THE RAT, sinking back in his seat again." Rat and Mole, the heroes of the classic children's story *The Wind in the Willows* by Kenneth Grahame, are out looking for a young otter who had gone missing when suddenly Rat sits up to listen to faint and fleeting music in the air. "'So beautiful and strange and new! Since it was to end so soon, I almost wish I had never heard it. For it has roused a longing in me that is pain, and nothing seems worth while but just to hear that sound once more and go on listening to it for ever. No! There it is again!' he cried, alert once more."

This confused Mole, since he could not yet hear the music. "I hear nothing myself," he said.

"O Mole! the beauty of it! The merry bubble and joy, the thin, clear, happy call of the distant piping! Such music I never dreamed of, and the call in it is stronger even than the music is sweet! Row on, Mole, row! For the music and the call must be for us."

Rat was captured by the music, transfixed on this new divine sound. He was "a powerless but happy infant in a strong sustaining grasp."

Mole continued to row, watching his companion tremble with joy and fear. Then Mole stopped rowing. Rat saw that now his confused friend began to hear it as well. The music "caught him up and possessed him utterly." They sat still in the boat, as the water led them, and the music began to "impose its will" on them.

As they began to float closer to the source, Rat whispers, "This is the place of my song-dream, the place the music played to me. Here, in this holy place, here if anywhere, surely we shall find Him!"[1]

Then suddenly the Mole felt a great Awe fall upon him, an awe that turned his muscles to water, bowed his head, and rooted his feet to the ground. It was no panic terror—indeed he felt wonderfully at peace and happy—but it was an awe that smote and held him and, without seeing, he knew it could only mean that some august Presence was very, very near. With difficulty he turned to look for his friend, and saw him at his side, cowed, stricken, and trembling violently. And still there was utter silence in the populous bird-haunted branches around them; and still the light grew and grew.

Perhaps he would never have dared to raise his eyes, but that, though the piping was now hushed, the call and the summons seemed still dominant and imperious. He might not refuse, were Death himself waiting to strike him instantly, once he had looked with mortal eye on things rightly kept hidden. Trembling he obeyed, and raised his humble head; and then, in that utter clearness of the imminent dawn, while Nature, flushed with fulness of incredible colour, seemed to hold her breath for the event, he looked in the very eyes of the Friend and Helper. . . . All this he saw, for one moment breathless and intense, vivid on the morning sky; and still, as he looked, he lived; and still, as he lived, he wondered.

"Rat!" he found breath to whisper, shaking. "Are you afraid?"

"Afraid?" murmured the Rat, his eyes shining with unutterable love. "Afraid! Of *Him*? O, never, never! And yet— and yet—O, Mole, I am afraid!"

Then the two animals, crouching to the earth, bowed their heads and did worship.[1]

This is one of my favorite sections of writing in all of literature. Grahame is showing us a joyful experience of the divine. Such experiences are best when we give up control and let ourselves be stricken by Awe itself and utterly imposed upon.

If you have been a Christian for some time, maybe this story evokes memories for you: memories of a time of corporate singing, when a line of an old hymn that had always seemed dusty and archaic was suddenly filled with good news and hope, and tears streamed down your face and the presence of Christ seemed to fill your chest. Or memories of a season of prayer when every word you read from Scripture felt like a burning bush, penetrating your heart with the conviction of sins but also with the warmth of forgiveness. Maybe there was a moment when you were taking the Lord's Supper and you felt as if Christ himself was breaking the bread and offering the cup, saying, "This is my body broken *for you* . . . my blood spilt *for you*." Before, those words felt rote, but suddenly they felt like eternal life.

For many of us, those experiences were more intense and frequent early in our life of faith. At the beginning, explosions of new insight and comfort seem to fall from every Bible story and sermon. But now maybe that has changed. *What has happened to my spiritual life?* we may ask. Prayer leads to boredom, worship leads to distraction, and all our attempts to change fall flat. Heightened experiences of joy seem to come in increments farther and farther apart.

Spiritual boredom and distraction are not new phenomena. They did not arrive with the advent of the internet. Christian leaders from the ancient church fathers to pastors today have been concerned about dealing with spiritual boredom and distraction. Henri Nouwen says that our minds are often "a banana tree filled with monkeys" when we try to sit and be still in prayer.[2] The old Egyptian monk Abba Agathon wrote, "For every time a man wants to pray, his enemies, the demons, want to prevent, for they know that it is only by turning him from prayer that they can hinder his journey."[3]

Another ancient Christian monk, John Cassian, put it this way,

For the character of the soul is not inappropriately compared to a light feather or plume. If it has not been harmed or spoiled by some liquid coming from outside, thanks to its inherent lightness it is naturally borne to the heavenly heights by the slightest of breath. But if it has been weighed down by a sprinkling or an outpouring of some liquid, not only will it not be borne off by its natural lightness and snatched up into the air, but it will even be pressed down to the lowest places on the earth by the weight of the liquid that it has taken on.[4]

We sit down to pray and we feel what weighs us down more than what transports us to glory. Distracted and bored, we feel as if we've forgotten how to pray and wonder if any of it was ever real.

Think of what the Israelites must have felt after they were delivered from slavery and had just reached the other side of the Red Sea. God had miraculously freed them from slavery. There was no denying it. They had all experienced it. Before their very eyes, the mighty Nile turned red with blood, frogs invaded, hail fell, locusts consumed, and the firstborn of the enemy were slaughtered while their own children were kept safe. They had been delivered through the blood of the first Passover lamb. They had passed through the Red Sea safely and heard the sound of their enemies drowning in judgment. Now they were on their way to a new country with the promise that God would be with them until they arrived in that new home.

What confidence they must have had! The songs they sang on the other side of the Red Sea were joyous. God's great salvation was fresh in their hearts.

But the wilderness awaited them. From Egypt to Canaan was a one-year journey, but God turned it into a forty-year pilgrimage because of their disobedience. The months and years that followed the Red Sea were filled with spiritual boredom.

Consider a scene from Israel's stay at Sinai. Moses had been gone a long time on top of the mountain to receive instruction on how they were to live as a new people (Exodus 24–31). There was much to communicate, for much change is needed for a people to live free when they've known only slavery. Moses climbed the mountain and left the people to their restlessness and desert boredom.

What happened next didn't result from a charlatan entering the camp promoting foreign gods or diverting the trust of the people from the Lord. It just took the people experiencing boredom. They wanted something—*anything*—to happen. But Moses wouldn't come down, and they were left with their questions and boredom.

I wonder if you've ever experienced these questions. What's going on with my life? I remember when things used to be so sweet. So much fruit, so much joy, so much life. Now there's nothing but mundanity.

When we're left to our restlessness, the key question comes: Has God forgotten me? Maybe I need to make something happen? At such times, we aren't sad, depressed, or even persecuted. There's just nothing.

In such boredom we reach for our idols—something to get things going again. "Come, Aaron, make us gods who will go before us!" And they put together an ad hoc god—a calf made of every earring and bracelet they could find and put into the fire (Exodus 32). Sure, that god might not have been beautiful or majestic, but it was a god on their terms. I can imagine them thinking, *The God of Moses seems to do things at his own pace and on his own terms. We need a god who works for us.* It didn't matter to them that the god they made seemed to be jury-rigged.

We can put up with a lot of dissatisfaction with our idols as long as they're working on our terms. Have you ever noticed that? The God of Moses seems to do as he pleases. He comes and goes when he wants. We are at his mercy. The idols, ridiculous, ugly, and thrown together as they are, are our gods and do as we please. We're tired of a God whose Spirit blows where it wishes (John 3:8). We're tired of waiting. We're tired of nothing, day after day. In our own ways, we cry out, "Make us gods, Aaron!"

Yet the wilderness of spiritual life is where maturity begins to take root. Psalm 92 gives us an image to consider.

> The righteous flourish like the palm tree
>   and grow like a cedar in Lebanon.
> They are planted in the house of the LORD;
>   they flourish in the courts of our God.
> They still bear fruit in old age. (Psalm 92:12-14)

This is what mature Christians are like: they are planted, they flourish, grow, and bear fruit—even in their old age. The remarkable thing about a tree growing, flourishing, and bearing fruit is that there are a lot of quiet moments, days, and years of fruitfulness. Waiting is boring—but it's where depth takes root.

The wilderness of spiritual boredom is dangerous terrain, full of temptations to remember old lusts. We get nostalgic for old slave masters. "Remember how good it was!" But a new kind of growth and spiritual strength comes when we wait amid the boredom. We pray and long, looking and waiting for God, as the watchman waits for the morning (Psalm 130:6). A watchman has nothing to do but wait and watch—but he's the first to see the light. Spiritual maturity and deep joy come when we learn to wait.

The Israelites hadn't learned how to wait for the God of Moses to come down the mountain. They quickly assumed they had been abandoned, left to die in the wilderness. So they took their lives into their own hands. Christians must learn to say, "No. We will wait here. Remember all that God has done. He will come down the mountain and into the valley with us again."

I remember sitting with a woman who was frustrated with her prayer life. She is a leader in our church, a spiritual mother, and a giant in the land, but she was confused. Flustered at the feeling of emptiness in prayer despite her consistent, daily effort, she felt like giving up. Where was the warmth? Where was the comfort? Where was the life?

Her daily practice was to get up early to read and pray. Then she would go to the gym before heading off to work. But she found that these days she was more interested in preparing for the gym and getting ahead on email than sitting down to pray. Her mind wandered to the tasks of the day or a difficult conversation she'd had. She was like a banana tree full of monkeys. What had happened?

We wondered together. Was she anxious? No. Was she depressed? No. There is a tendency to feel as if we've done something wrong when this happens. To be sure, there are habits that keep us from attentive prayer. Some distraction and boredom come from weeds of desire that need to be pulled from the heart for stability and strength in prayer.

Sometimes, though, there's something deeper at work. We simply need to wait. "Be still before the LORD and wait patiently for him; fret not yourself over the one who prospers in his way" (Psalm 37:7). Waiting is one of the least effective things we can imagine doing. Not much is getting accomplished when we wait—but waiting is often the key toward spiritual fruitfulness.

My friend wasn't slouching toward spiritual immaturity, quite the opposite. She was experiencing the pains of maturity. Before, she had experienced the "ask, and it will be given to you" presence of Christ (Matthew 7:7), but now she was experiencing a mysterious absence.

In his book *Sacred Fire*, Ronald Rolheiser relates this experience to moving past the honeymoon stage of marriage. Moving past the honeymoon stage doesn't indicate a bad marriage, but it does mean you must shift and embody this new relational dynamic with your spouse in order to be faithful, not just merely long for the old days. When you're dating and early in marriage, your love is full of strong emotions and passions. This person is *enough* for you. He or she fills you and takes away your loneliness. The energy produced by your beloved's presence is exciting. "You complete me" isn't just a silly line from a romance movie but a witness to what we really *want* to say to the other person when we are honeymooning. *What more could I want?*

But at some point you realize that you really did marry just one singular person who has limitations. Habits set in and life comes back into focus. You have not fallen out of love, Rolheiser says, but out of your own fantasy of love. Now you will have to love the mundane spouse, not just the honeymoon spouse. Love becomes more than an explosion in the sky, choosing to be present with your spouse in the very normal moments for the rest of your life.

> When the honeymoon dies, the big dream is over and we realize that we can defy gravity and make love to the whole world only in our dreams, because in reality our lives come down to this singular person, this singular family, this one city, this too-small house, this less-than-fulfilling job, this irritating mortgage, these non-famous friends, and this less-than-perfect-body. Reality has broken through and we see a very limited horizon at the end of the tunnel.[5]

It's not that there aren't still fireworks after ten years of marriage or after the second or third child. It's just that the fireworks must come through mundane, choosing-to-be-present moments of love with the other, not through a life that resists such moments. In the same way, maturity, depth, and stability in prayer come through mundane, choosing-to-be-present moments with Christ, not a life that resists them. "Be still before the LORD, and wait patiently for him."

Entering into this new season with Christ, we have to admit that maybe we enjoyed the feelings of what the Lord gave in prayer more than the Lord himself. We have to learn to pray in this new maturity that the Lord is leading us into. Rolheiser calls this not a crisis of faith but a crisis of imagination.[6] He provides the example of how the disciples experienced Christ on the road to Emmaus (Luke 24). Christ was crucified, buried, and risen again. Two disciples who had heard rumors of his resurrection were traveling to Emmaus. They were discouraged— they had only imagined the Christ who fed the five thousand, who performed the healings, and who taught with such authority. The crucifixion was a major disillusionment.

While they were walking, the risen Jesus met them on the road, but they did not recognize him. They knew the popular, crowd-stirring Christ, not the crucified and resurrected Christ.

> A crucified Jesus did not fit into [their] understanding and thus was unrecognizable to them, even as he was chatting with them. This is an experience that we will all undergo at various times during our adult lives: for all of us there will come times when everything that is precious to us religiously will get crucified and we will find ourselves discouraged, shattered religiously, and tempted to walk toward some place of consolation.[7]

As we mature, our Father invites us to reimagine our spiritual life with the Jesus of the Emmaus Road. Previously, we knew the Christ of great experiences and emotions. Now, mundane spiritual moments and longing for a second honeymoon have come.

A deeper, more profound love and romance with my wife will not only include heightened emotions and pleasure, but it will have to include the moments of exhaustion, where after a day of our children's dentist appointments and mind-numbing meetings, we are sitting next to one another on the couch with a glass of wine, talking through our day, and waiting to go to bed. There may be few fireworks in these moments, but there is potential for depth of companionship, even in these mundane moments of weariness—or *especially* in these moments.

Joy comes, however. "Did not our hearts burn within us while he talked to us on the road, while he opened to us the Scriptures?"

(Luke 24:32), the disciples asked after Jesus left. There was now a deeper passion and a more profound encounter with Christ. This "burning of the heart" often comes at us sideways and indirectly. These sustaining experiences and joy come not when we are looking for them but when we are looking *for him*. Often the burning heart comes through confusion, questions, dryness, and boredom—but on the other side is friendship, intimacy, and, yes, ecstasy.

Psalm 91 is a song of confidence.

> He will deliver you from the snare of the fowler. . . .
> He will cover you with his pinions,
>> and under his wings you will find refuge;
>> his faithfulness is a shield and buckler.
> You will not fear the terror of the night,
>> nor the arrow that flies by day,
> nor the pestilence that stalks in darkness,
>> nor the destruction that wastes at noonday. (vv. 3-6)

The Lord is a refuge and protector for this psalmist. His confidence comes from somewhere down deep.

> A thousand may fall at your side,
>> ten thousand at your right hand,
>> but it will not come near you. (v.7)

This is amazing confidence. Even if he's speaking with a bit of poetic hyperbole, it is still quite bold. Even when a thousand, no, *ten thousand* fall beside me, I will not fall with them. Where does this almost cocky confidence come from?

> He who dwells in the shelter of the Most High
>> will abide in the shadow of the Almighty. (v. 1)

This experiential comfort and stability is based on the behavior of this first line of the song, *dwelling* and *abiding*. These are serious words. They run throughout all the books of Scripture, and they are concerned with promises of God being *with* us. From the fire and smoke of the wilderness wanderings of the exodus to the incarnation of Christ in the Gospels, God promises to be with his people—and his people will be with him, dwelling and abiding.

These are words about life, about rootedness. The psalmist is like a cedar tree with roots down deep into the earth. It bears fruit even into old age, dwelling and abiding in the ground. This doesn't happen to a person overnight or in a week. It happens over time and through seasons.

The word *dwelling* is concerned with home, and the word *abiding* is concerned with relationships. "Abide in me," Jesus says in John 15. "Abide in me, and I in you" (v. 4). "If you abide in me, and my words abide in you, ask whatever you wish, and it will be done for you" (v. 7). That last part of verse 7 is what people pay attention to, "ask whatever you wish!" But the first part is the key, "If you abide in me, and my words abide in you." It means that we are with Christ more than at the times when we ask for things. In other words, our abiding is more characteristic than our asking, so eventually our asking becomes more informed by our abiding.

But *dwelling* and *abiding* are mundane words. This is the danger that tempts us to move away. We move away from a place because "Nothing happens here!" I pastor in a city full of people running away from places where "nothing ever happens" to try to make *something* happen. So they move to New York!

But the psalmist has learned that the secret to stability and courage is dwelling and abiding; it's in the quiet, mundane seasons that our roots stretch farther into the ground.

This counterintuitive wisdom teaches us that the mornings of yawning through our prayers are more important than we think. That is what dwelling and abiding look like! I have often thought to myself, *What a waste! I could have slept another thirty minutes instead of blinking through my reading.*

Resist this conclusion. The things we value are the things worth yawning and blinking through. Something more than intellectual exercise and reading comprehension is happening in prayer. We are dwelling and abiding. Yes, it's mundane, often slow, and sometimes confusing. But this is what it teaches us to say, "Ten thousand may fall at my side, but it will not come near me!"

The church fathers had a term for seasons of dryness: *educative desolation*. Diadochos of Photiki from the fifth century says that God uses *educative desolation* to draw our spirit forward to him. God withholds the sweetness of his light so we will long again for him. He hides the "experience of divine attention" in order to increase our joy and desire in him.[8] This is a humbling experience, but we find it all through the Psalms:

> How long, O LORD? Will you forget me forever?
>> How long will you hide your face from me?
> How long must I take counsel in my soul
>> and have sorrow in my heart all the day? (Psalm 13:1-2)

I'm thankful that God chose to inspire words like these. There is grief—and humiliation—in these words. They're almost accusatory.

If the spiritual giants of the psalms can experience divine absence, how much more can we? God knows we will reach this place, and he has given us words to say when we get there. "Here," he says, "use these words. They will help."

The soul that "seeks glory and is easily exalted," Diadochos says, "does not easily renew its love of God."[9] And so God wisely leads us into seasons of maturity. But he leaves bread crumbs in Psalms that tell us that others have been here before us. We are in good company, even here in this darkness.

Early in our faith we have a tendency to see our experiences of amazement as maturity. But the New Testament calls us to be suspicious of our amazement.[10] The crowds that were amazed at the miracles of Jesus and crying "Hosanna!" as he entered Jerusalem on a donkey, were crying "Crucify him!" just a few days later.

The opposite of this kind of amazement, Rolheiser says, is pondering. Our spiritual maturity will ask for more pondering than amazement.

> Amazement lies at the root of hype, ideology, groupthink, mob mentality, gang rapes, and crucifixions. . . . To ponder, biblically, is the opposite of this. We ponder when we do not let the energy of the crowd or spontaneous emotion simply flow through us and become the basis for our actions. Instead we hold and carry and transform that energy so as to not mindlessly retransmit it. And this capacity lies at the root of deeper maturity and deeper virtue.[11]

Mary is the hero of the pondering stories in the Gospels. While everyone around her is stirred and amazed, she ponders all these things in her heart (Luke 2:19). Some translations use *treasured*. I like that too, but it has the danger of communicating nostalgia to us modern readers, as if Mary kept these memories of angels and wise men to look back on and treasure. It doesn't mean that. It means that she took in all the data of that moment and let it into her heart and kept it there so it might transform and change her.

Our prayers are often like this biblical amazement. "We simply let energy flow through," Rolheiser writes,

> in the same way as a wire conducts an electrical current, when we simply take in the energy of the group around us or the energy of spontaneous emotion and, without holding, carrying, or transforming it, act on it as it flows through us. That can sometimes be harmless or even good, at a rock concert or a football game, but it can also be mindless, negative, and dangerous.[12]

We need to find ways of slowing down and pondering, sitting with the words of Psalms, the Gospels, and Paul so they might fill us and change us.

In our prayers and readings of Scripture there will be moments that cause amazement, as if glory incarnate reaches out from the pages to grab us. But not every prayer or every reading will do this. If a spiritual leader tells you that all your encounters with God should be like Mount Sinai, then either that leader has not been praying for long or is trying to sell you something. Not every prayer will lead to amazement, but every prayer deserves our pondering. Waiting on the Lord means our experiences of joy and ecstasy come on his terms. We must be present for all of it, for the mundane and for the glorious.

THE PRACTICE
of PRAYER

IN 1950 THE ATHEIST PHILOSOPHER Bertrand Russell received the Nobel Prize. In his acceptance speech he talked about human desire in words that just as easily might have come from St. Augustine. "All human activity is prompted by desire," he said.

None of us want to admit this. We want to think of ourselves as truly rational, composed, and not controlled by our desires but Russell says we can't escape it. There are some, he went on, who believe "it is possible to resist desire in the interests of duty and moral principle." The problem with that belief is not that a person never acts out of duty but that "duty has no hold on him unless he desires to be dutiful." Russell continues,

> If you wish to know what men will do, you must know not only, or principally, their material circumstances, but rather the whole system of their desires with their relative strengths. . . . Man differs from other animals in one very important respect, and that is that he has some desires which are, so to speak,

infinite, which can never be fully gratified, and which would keep him restless even in Paradise. The boa constrictor, when he has had an adequate meal, goes to sleep, and does not wake until he needs another meal. Human beings, for the most part, are not like this.[1]

He's right. Our behavior is driven by what we desire—what we love. This can be a frustrating reality because there is a great division between who we want to be and how we actually live. We want to be one way, but something deeper is directing our behavior. There are deeper desires at work that we are often unconscious of but are still driving what we do.

Have you ever wondered why you can't kick a particular habit? Why you're so impatient? Why you're so afraid? Why can't you ever seem to change? Scripture and human history show us that we are driven by deeper hungers—desires that are infinite and keep us restless, as Russell says. We need deeper mechanisms of change.

Prayer changes us by shrinking the gap between who we are and who we long to become in Christ. We are neither saved nor sanctified by good habits, but certain habits put us in the way of transformation and change.

Part one was on the possibility of prayer; part two is on its practice. The practice of prayer consists of primary rhythms (communion, meditation, and solitude), and secondary rhythms (Sabbath resting, fasting and feasting, and corporate worship). The word *secondary* shouldn't communicate "optional" or even "supplemental." Just as faith without works is dead and love without truth is trivial, primary and secondary rhythms of prayer depend on one another for vibrancy and life. Our personal times of communion, meditation, and solitude are enhanced by the regular rhythms of Sabbath rest, fasting and feasting, and corporate worship. And our rhythms of Sabbath rest, fasting and feasting, and corporate worship are deepened by our personal habits of communion, meditation, and solitude. What God has joined together, let no human put asunder!

I said at the beginning of part one that prayer is not a matter of technique. Instead, there are realities we need to grasp that lead to pathways, rather than techniques, toward intimacy with God. In part one we considered the realities. In part two we see the pathways.

CHAPTER SEVEN

COMMUNION

THROUGHOUT THE CENTURIES Christians have used the word *communion* to emphasize the relational side of prayer. Communion is the act of nurturing a loving relationship with God. Ronald Rolheiser describes it as "getting close enough to God to hear him say 'I love you.'"[1] It is opening yourself up to God, believing that he has opened himself up to you. Communion becomes transformative when it becomes a regular rhythm of our lives.

Communion is a transformative habit, but personal transformation cannot be the ultimate goal or it will never be transformative. God must never be a mere enhancement to our self-improvement plan or a ticket to a better life. He is life itself. He must be the goal, the end, the prize. Communion is coming to God for the sake of God: for his beauty, his love, his presence, his joy. But transformation slips in through the backdoor and comes at us sideways. We are changed indirectly by our enjoyment of God.

Psalm 34 helps us imagine what communion with God looks like. There are at least five elements revealed in this psalm that help us put it into practice: boasting, seeking, enjoying, showing, and being.

BOASTING

I will bless the LORD at all times;
  his praise shall continually be in my mouth.
My soul makes its boast in the LORD;
  let the humble hear and be glad.
Oh, magnify the LORD with me,
  and let us exalt his name together! (Psalm 34:1-3)

The psalmist, King David, begins with boasting. His heart is so full of the loveliness of God that he is moved to call others to participate: "Oh, magnify the Lord with me!" Like a beautiful sunset that compels you to call someone to come and see, these things are better experienced with others.

"My soul makes its boast in the LORD." *Boasting* is important for communion. We boast in what we treasure: "Look at what I have here!" We boast in our strengths: "Look at what I can do!" We boast in our accomplishments: "Look at what I've done!" We boast in our associations: "Look at who I know!" For David, his boast is in the Lord: his treasure, his strength, his greatest association.

Communion is the act of pushing what is most lovely— God—to the center of our desires. The center of our life has become our Beloved. David is using this portion of his prayer to enlarge his heart and consider all the preciousness of God. Look at what he's done! Look at who he is!

After you read a passage of Scripture, write down or take note of what the passage says about God, his beauty, his power, his faithfulness, his love, his presence, his glory, his grace, and his majesty. Sit with these truths and let them move around in your heart, pushing to the side smaller things that often demand your attention. This can be for a few brief moments, or it can take up your entire prayer time. Speak of your love for him. Say to him, simply, "I love you."

This work of boasting and adoring in communion is a *counter-habit*. The normal bent of our hearts is to magnify ourselves. Our natural, selfish, inward orientation is our main obstacle to fullness, and our society seeks to indulge this impulse—to think and marvel at ourselves first. It is the archenemy of spiritual vibrancy and growth. Boasting in the Lord is a counterhabit that begins to shape our prayer into a communion of love.

Our society teaches us what we ought to value, what we ought to be sorry about, and how can we find hope. We have personal habits and rhythms that enforce these beliefs. Like rushing water slowly forming grooves in a rock over time, our hearts have created ways of thinking, believing, living, and loving by these habits and rhythms. No one becomes consumeristic by reading a pamphlet on consumerism and being convinced of its arguments. Instead, we allow habits of spending to shape what we love.

Boasting in God is a habit that slowly creates different grooves in our heart, new affections, new loves. It's a counter-habit as well to those of us who, when we are honest, offer more complaint and grumbling than praise and thanksgiving. But in adoration we realize that continual praise, blessing the Lord at all times, and boasting in him is simply thinking straight! He's God. He's worthy of it. He's our Redeemer, Savior, Refuge, Comforter, Friend! If I'm thinking straight, of course praise comes out.

SEEKING

I sought the LORD, and he answered me
and delivered me from all my fears.
Those who look to him are radiant,
and their faces shall never be ashamed. (Psalm 34:4-5)

Seeking the Lord is not just asking something of God. In Hebrew, *seeking* is a relationally heavy word. It has elements of waiting, listening, and speaking. It suggests face-to-face conversation. Do we think of prayer like that? As seeking out a face-to-face exchange? "I sought the LORD," David says, "and he answered me." Back and forth—prayer is a dialogue.

That means that we will need *time* to listen. How often do we listen in prayer? Would you characterize any part of your spiritual life as "listening"? Communion is a relationship. To pray is to nurture a loving relationship—to get close enough to God to hear him say "I love you" and to say it back.

"Prayer does not seek to draw God toward us," St. Augustine says, "he is closer to us than we are to ourselves. Its purpose is to bring us close enough to him for dialogue, and to make us aware of his nearness." Communion, Olivier Clément says, is "the correspondence between the depths of the heart and the heights of heaven."² Communion seeks out divine company, and heaven responds with "yes." To seek is to long for nearness. "A single word in intimacy is worth more than a thousand at a distance," says Evagrius of Pontus.³

"Those who look to him are radiant" (Psalm 34:5). If you've ever wondered why some people seem to have a spiritual radiance about them, this is why. Those who seek him are radiant, "and their faces shall never be ashamed." Whatever we seek, that is what we will become like. "Those who make [false idols] become like them," we read in another psalm, "so do all who trust in them" (Psalm 115:8).

Psalm 115 is a warning. We become like whatever we worship and seek. If it's lots of money, the spirit of greed and consumerism will shape us into its likeness. If it's a successful career, we will become image bearers of ambition and power. These idols have no hands to save us, no eyes to see us, and no mouth to speak words of true comfort. Our trust in them makes us like them: weak, blind, deaf, and dumb—numb to ultimate reality and beauty.

But those who seek the Lord "are radiant." The Hebrew word here literally means "a radiant face," an allusion to the story of Moses in Exodus 33–34. Moses was on a mountain with God, desperate to see God's glory. The Lord knew that an unfiltered glance at his divine radiance would kill Moses, so he allowed Moses a side-glance rather than a direct look. But even that was enough to light up Moses' face. His face became so radiant that the people could not look at it, so he wore a veil. Moses sought the Lord's glory, and with a divine wink the Lord turned Moses' face into a sun.

In 2 Corinthians, Paul picks up this theme. He says that when we pray with our Bibles open and meditate on Scripture, what happened to Moses' face happens to our hearts: "We all, with unveiled face, beholding the glory of the Lord, are being transformed into the same image from one degree of glory to another. For this comes from the Lord who is the Spirit" (2 Corinthians 3:18). Those who seek him are radiant.

Seeking the Lord looks like reading and praying with intentionality, employing the inner desire to know and hear him. Set aside distractions. Turn off phones. Put aside work and email. Close your door and seek him with the eyes of your heart. "Seek, and you will find; knock, and the door will be opened to you" (Luke 11:9). That means we do not let our reading or praying become rote or mindless. We seek him, calling our hearts to give him our attention.

ENJOYING

Oh, taste and see that the LORD is good!
  Blessed is the man who takes refuge in him!
Oh, fear the LORD, you his saints,
  for those who fear him have no lack!
The young lions suffer want and hunger;
  but those who seek the LORD lack no good thing.
    (Psalm 34:8-10)

In John 1, when Jesus' new disciples had questions about him, his answer was an invitation: "Come and you will see" (John 1:39). While Jesus often resisted giving plain answers, he always invited people to experience alongside him what was ahead, and the answers often came as they went along. David is not so much explaining what spiritual vibrancy is as inviting us to experience it. Taste and see.

Notice the sensory language: taste, see. Isn't that interesting? Our hearts hunger and thirst too, and if we do not look to God to satisfy them, we will look to something else. We are desire-oriented creatures. Augustine says we have infinite hunger, and God is infinite fullness. David is instructing us to aim our desires at God in prayer, pressing near to enjoy him. Don't settle for lesser foods.

David is describing a spiritual life that reads Scripture with the taste buds of your heart. It's a command to enjoy, to taste the goodness. Come near, enlarge your heart. "Open your mouth wide, and I will fill it" (Psalm 81:10). Christianity is a desire-oriented religion. We are meant—commanded!—to pursue delight and pleasure. Does that surprise you? The only rebuke is against finding delight in things that aren't meant to satisfy the "infinite hunger" Augustine talks about.

The psalmist bears witness: I have tasted and seen. I have opened my mouth wide, and he has filled it. It's true. Do you believe him? God is satisfying. We are meant to come back again and again for our enjoyment. We will lack no good thing.

Enjoying God is a learned habit. This kind of delight reaches to the deep parts of our heart, a place that we do not often use, frankly. The muscles down there are weak, and it takes time to build them up. But David's witness stirs us to keep going. It will take some maturing of our heart's palate. If we have grown accustomed to foods that are superficially sweet, good food—with complex and subtle flavors—can taste bland or bitter. But if we refrain from sugary foods for a while, we begin to experience flavors we hadn't noticed before. Once our palate has been cleansed and we've experienced the depth of flavors on offer, it's less appealing to go back.

If we spend our heart's desire on the small, glittery things in this world, communion with God can seem mundane and even boring. Our taste buds aren't developed enough yet. Incidentally, this is one of the benefits of fasting—it clears the palate of our hearts and prepares us for the richness of the presence of God.

SHOWING

"Come, O children, listen to me; I will teach you the fear of the LORD" (Psalm 34:11). David turns to address his listeners and readers. "Come listen to me and I will teach you." It's a father-child, a mentor-student relationship, where someone who is further along in the faith joins someone who recognizes a need for growth. These relationships have been going on since the beginning. Some traditions call this relationship "spiritual direction." It's an intentional relationship where one person voluntarily submits the direction of their spiritual life to another, listening and learning. The Lord uses these relationships to enrich the communion of both parties. The teacher has riches to share, and in the sharing, the student is lifted and the teacher grows deeper.

Isn't that a beautiful thing? If you share wisdom with me from your spiritual life, I'll have more wisdom than I did before, but you won't have less. Something wonderful has been multiplied. Creation has occurred. Knowledge of holy things has spread from your heart to mine. It has been planted in me even as it grows deeper in you.

I can recall times when I shared something that has been fruitful for me in the past, and in doing so I recognized that I needed to rediscover what I had just passed along.

Sometimes teaching on an element of prayer enhances my own experience of it. Teaching or sharing allows me the opportunity for deeper reflection.

We all need to grow in prayer and spiritual vibrancy. There's a good chance that's the reason you are reading this book, for which I'm glad. But books can't teach us everything we need to know. You need to find friends a few steps ahead of you in the faith and ask them to teach you to pray. Let them show you. Let them tell you what they've experienced, how they struggle. Seek them out. Offer to buy them breakfast or coffee once or twice a month for a while. Submit your spiritual life to their direction for a season. That's a good discipline.

Some of us need to begin to act like mothers and fathers toward others. Maybe you've been a Christian for a long time, and while you may not feel spiritually elite, you have had a fruitful prayer life for some time. Find someone who needs to grow in prayer. Invest in their joy and spiritual life. It will grow you along the way.

While some of us can be a spiritual mother or father to others, none of us have grown out of needing help. We will never test out of the necessity for our own spiritual director. I have people in my life who speak into my prayer practices. When I'm getting indulgent, they show me a better way. When I'm sad, they encourage me to consider trying something that has helped them in their own times of sadness. Many of my friends—those who are older or farther along—have wrestled with prayer and found fullness through many different practices and have encouraged me toward paths of intimacy I hadn't experienced before.

Some years back my wife and I discovered what is now one of our favorite books, *The Supper of the Lamb* by Robert Farrar Capon. It's a culinary reflection on joy and life. It's a cookbook, but it's also theology. Capon is funny but also aims to rescue us from the dangers of mediocrity in our eating life, where there's so much pleasure to be found—even in cutting an onion! My wife and I found the book and we both wanted to read it. So over several evenings, we shared a bottle of wine and took turns reading it out loud to one another. We had so much fun. There were moments when we had to put our glasses down because we had to belly laugh or stop to consider and reread what was just said. "Underline that!" we would say. Those moments stirred intimacy and vibrancy in us.

Now, with some years of marriage under our belt, we often suggest something like that to a couple struggling to connect their hearts. "Pick up a bottle, get some nice bread, and read this wonderful book out loud to each other!" we often say.

Wine that gladdens human hearts,
    oil to make their faces shine,
    and bread that sustains their hearts.
    (Psalm 104:15 NIV)

Bread for strength, wine for joy, and Robert Capon to make your face shine. It's not a marriage technique we are trying to peddle; it's a pathway to intimacy we've discovered. Maybe it can help others along the way.

That's what I mean by a spiritual director, not someone who's trying to peddle new prayer techniques but who has experienced pathways of intimacy you can try on and make your own as you seek communion with God. We need others who know God, who have traveled the terrain of prayer, who have seen other views and discovered other vistas. We need friends who have pursued disciplines and habits in ways we haven't and have experienced healing in ways we need.

BEING

The psalmist declares,

> The eyes of the LORD are toward the righteous
>   and his ears toward their cry.
> The face of the LORD is against those who do evil,
>   to cut off the memory of them from the earth.
> When the righteous cry for help, the LORD hears
>   and delivers them out of all their troubles.
>   (Psalm 34:15-17)

For some of us, Psalm 34 sounds wonderful until we get to verse 15, where the eyes of the Lord are toward the righteous. It's when "the *righteous* cry for help" that the Lord hears. And we wonder, does that include me? Have I been applying this psalm to my life when it's really reserved for the more holy among us?

Here's where a theology of Psalms is important to have tucked into your consciousness as you read. Righteous is less about a moral standard we keep and more about a living fellowship with God that we've been given. A righteous person has access to God, and God listens. It's someone with a living relationship with God. Scripture shows us that we receive righteous status when we are *in Christ*. Our faith in Christ puts us *in*

Christ and brings us into fellowship with God. It's a new status that comes with faith. It isn't based on moral accomplishments but on the life and death of Christ. Everything we receive is based on the merits of Christ, not our own. Our status with the Father is the same as the status of Christ with the Father.

So the potential of prayer is that the same joy, the same benefits, and the same strength that Christ himself enjoys and receives in his relationship with the Father are available to us *in Christ*. The same power to resist temptation, to love, and to sacrifice that was available to Christ is available to us.

There's a voice that tempts us to believe that these prayers are reserved for the righteous few. But the Spirit of Christ whispers to us that these are our prayers, meant for us to pray and take comfort in. "The LORD is near to the brokenhearted and saves the crushed in spirit" (Psalm 34:18). That's a wonderful promise, and it's ours.

CHAPTER EIGHT

MEDITATION

"I DO NOT UNDERSTAND MY OWN ACTIONS" (Romans 7:15). The apostle Paul sums up much of the Christian experience in this short sentence. I am a mystery to myself. "I do the very thing I hate," Paul goes on to say. I am a bag of contradictions.

Do you resonate with that? Most Christians who have grown in self-awareness see this in their own lives. They see the gap between who they want to be and how they behave, between what they know to be true and what they experience. Sometimes the gap between the two can be discouraging. I don't only mean the gap between righteous living and moral failure. I also mean the gap between our confidence in Christ and the experience of hopelessness.

The work of maturity and growth makes the gap between what we know and how we live smaller. Much of the work is done mysteriously, hidden in the inner parts of our lives by the presence of Christ. Our part is to daily put ourselves in the way of that work of transformation. A life of prayer puts us in the most concentrated path of that deep work. And one of the main parts of a life of prayer is the practice of meditation.

Psalms give us a model for meditation and an imagination for what is possible within us. The good thing about models is that they are not formulas. A formulaic prayer life is attractive because it promises to be simple, but in the end it turns out to be simplistic. Just follow these steps, 1-2-3, and *presto*! But formulaic prayers don't often make sense of the complexities of life or the distinctiveness of each of us. Formulas are tempting when we get impatient with the slowness of spiritual maturity. Formulas are good for producing commodities and merchandise but terrible for inner transformation.

A model is something we can try on, grow into, or reconfigure. Models are meant to be applied to our circumstances. They are dynamic. Models are guides that help us make sense of our condition. They provide guardrails so we don't feel lost along the way and we know how to keep moving, allowing for the complexity and uniqueness of our own lives and circumstances. The psalms give us a model of meditation. The model is not a combination to a locked door but a path toward the land of the living.

Psalm 77 is a good example of the model of meditation. It's split into two parts. Take an opportunity to read it. Part one (vv. 1-10) is what we might call dark poetry. It's a complaint—discouraged, hopeless, and exhausted. Asaph, the poet, is feeling abandoned by God. He is in trouble and has been crying out day and night, but God has not answered. Part two (vv. 11-20) is filled with praise and confidence. Now Asaph is joyful and full of hope. Verses 13-15 are intense praise and worship to the Lord.

The key to understanding this psalm is grasping what happened between parts one and two. How do we go from verse 9, "Has God forgotten to be gracious?" to verse 14, "You are the God who works wonders"? The key is that Asaph meditated on Scripture—the stories of God's character, love, presence, and faithfulness. Asaph put himself into the stories of God's work.

PRAYING WITH AN HONEST HEART

Every prayer has a context. Every morning has a day behind and ahead of it. For some of us yesterday provokes feelings of guilt or shame that we bring into our prayers, and for some of us the day ahead stirs fear. Every prayer is enfleshed by experiences that bring pain or excitement, hope or despair, fullness or emptiness. There are no disembodied prayers. Pretending there are leads to a shallow spiritual life.

Asaph the poet is not a pretender and has no patience for pretense. "My soul refuses to be comforted" (Psalm 77:2). He will not put up with false assurances that everything is okay when everything clearly is not. This psalm reveals anger and frustration, primarily against God. "In the day of my trouble I seek the Lord; in the night my hand is stretched out without wearying" (v. 2). But it's as if his prayers are hitting the ceiling and going no further. He experiences no comfort from the Lord. "Will the Lord spurn forever, and never again be favorable?" (v. 7). He begins to ask darker questions:

Has his steadfast love forever ceased?

Are his promises at an end for all times?

Has God forgotten to be gracious? (vv. 8-9)

Asaph is asking the question we often feel uncomfortable asking: Has God changed? His steadfast love does not feel steadfast. The Scriptures teach us that God's character is unchanging, that he is not capricious or temperamental. The psalmist is asking why his experiences do not match that truth.

We don't need to know exactly what Asaph was going through. It doesn't take a terribly long life to have experiences that provoke these kinds of questions. Maybe just reading this psalm conjures up such moments. Maybe you're in one right now. Asaph is going through trouble without any sense that God cares for him, and it makes him cold. Just thinking about God makes him moan (v. 3). He can't sleep, and it's God's fault (v. 4). In verses 5-6 he remembers when times were good. How did things get so bad?

These are dark questions for the author of an inspired psalm, but they are real questions. If you are going through real pain, confusion, and distress, these kinds of questions come to the surface. Where is God? Where are his promises? It's interesting that the psalmist is not asking for a different situation. He's just asking God to comfort him.

We need to bring an honest heart to God to receive what he has for us. Maybe you're full of apathy and spiritual lethargy. Maybe you're fearful of what lies ahead in life. Maybe you've been far away from God. Maybe you've been hurtful to others. Maybe you've committed some significant moral failures. Maybe you've experienced the loss of a spouse or friend. Maybe you've failed at something significant at work. Maybe you've experienced one disappointment after another. Come honestly and vulnerably to God with the emotions that come with those experiences. If you don't, you'll be numb to the gifts God has already given and the healing that is to come.

PRAYING WITH INTENTIONAL REMEMBRANCE

At verse 10, Psalm 77 takes a turn. "I will appeal to this, to the years of the right hand of the Most High." The "right hand" in Scripture is always an image of God's power. The psalmist observes,

> I will remember the deeds of the LORD;
>> yes, I will remember your wonders of old.
> I will ponder all your work,
>> and meditate on your mighty deeds. (vv. 11-12)

He is meditating on God's powerful work in the past, remembering that he has been the gracious beneficiary of that power.

There are four important verbs in verses 10-12: I will appeal, I will remember, I will ponder, and I will meditate. In Hebrew, there's a little vowel at the end of each of these verbs that adds intensity to them. Don't let the airy feel of the English words *ponder* and *meditate* fool you. The psalmist is not engaging in passive exercises. This is not the gentle emotional work of relaxing and trying to empty your mind. It's fighting. These are intentional habits: I *will* appeal; I *will* remember; I *will* ponder; I *will* meditate. Christian meditation is fighting, grasping for joy. It's intentionally and regularly remembering and pondering the history of God's power for his people. If you coast, you lose.

I will appeal. The psalmist has considered his own situation and asked some honest questions of God. Where has God been? Is he conscious of my pain? Does he care? And the psalmist has considered his circumstances and emotions in response to those questions. Now he's turning his attention to other things. He is appealing to the years, the history, of God's right hand.

This is an important move. The psalmist is not ignoring his emotions, but he doesn't want his prayers to be driven by them. So he turns to consider evidence outside his circumstances by remembering what God has done in the past. This means reading and recalling what God has done in the stories of Scripture. This isn't an impersonal, analytical move. Appealing to Scripture and the history of God's right hand is putting yourself in the stories not as a bystander but as a participant. "It is possible," Eugene Peterson writes, "to read the Bible from a number of different angles and for various purposes without dealing with God as God revealed himself, without setting ourselves under the authority of the Father, the Son, and the Holy Spirit who is alive and present in everything we are and do."[1] Getting involved with the story of Scripture is getting involved with God. What do you have for me, O Lord?

I will remember. Remembering is not merely bringing to mind, as in, "Oh that's right. I completely forgot God is gracious!" Rather, Asaph is reminding his heart of God's grace. He's remembering the promises of God and how God has been faithful in the past. Remembering is interpreting our circumstances (whether joyful or painful) through God's history and promises. What could God be doing? What is he trying to show me? What do I need to learn? Asaph goes back to a very famous story, the exodus. He remembers that the Lord made a path through the sea, and the Lord's people walked through on dry land to escape from their enemies (Psalm 77:19). He remembers that God led his people out of slavery into freedom (v. 20).

Remembering is not the same as nostalgia. Nostalgia looks at how great we were or how wonderful our circumstances were at one time—the freedom, the ease, the comfort. Nostalgia looks at the glory days. "Glory days," Bruce Springsteen says, "They'll pass you by."[2] But when we look at past mercies, we'll potentially have eyes to see the new ones. If we depend on nostalgia, we'll be disappointed and grow in bitterness when circumstances aren't what they were. Nostalgia is always hoping for less complicated days, seeking a haven of comfortable spirituality.[3] It drives us back to old slave masters, "We remember the fish we ate in Egypt that cost nothing, the cucumbers, the melons, the leeks, the onions, and the garlic" (Numbers 11:5). Of course, you ate at no cost! You were slaves!

I will ponder. To ponder is to draw out the significance of what we remember. It's not a relaxed action but an active one. What does the exodus mean? If this is true of God, how should I think? How should I believe? The psalmist asks questions of the text he's considering. What does this story say about God? What does it say about me? If he's pondering the exodus, what might he say?

The exodus tells the story of how the Israelite nation was once enslaved, at the mercy of someone greater than them, subjected to evil. But they were delivered because God loved them, chose them, and called them his "son." But they couldn't be arrogant. They weren't delivered because they were more virtuous. It was only grace, manifest in the Passover lamb. And God worked so many wonders! He split the seas for them, and they walked on dry land away from danger. If it hadn't been for God's continued power, they would have been brought back to slavery, or they might have gone back to slavery on their own initiative! And although they were in the wilderness, he was present with them and kept them safe until they got to their new home.

If you are a modern Christian, you might ponder the exodus story the same way. I was enslaved to sin and the flesh, but now I'm set free, delivered and made a child of God not because I was more virtuous than others or more righteous, but through the blood of the Lamb, by which God delivered up his only Son for me. He split the sea of judgment, and I walked on dry land to the other side, from death to life. He worked so many wonders to save me, the most significant being the resurrection. And although this life often feels like a wilderness, dangerous and desolate, he's present with me. He really is. I'm always tempted to go back into slavery. It would be easier. But he keeps me. He is keeping me until I make it to my new home.

I will meditate. So far, we've appealed, remembered, and pondered. These can be done simultaneously, maybe within ten to twenty minutes. The psalmist is telling us to read the text spiritually. We're not just reading the text to find examples to follow but mercies to receive. So far, we've come to the text asking what God has for us and how we can put ourselves in the way of receiving it. Now we gather all that up into meditation.

Meditation is the discipline that lights the fuse between the understanding of the mind and the tasting of the heart—the knowledge of God and the joy of his presence. Richard Baxter, a seventeenth-century pastor in England, said that meditation is to read the Bible in such a way as to make your heart hot. It turns your Bible readings into a burning bush.

While the text we read is thousands of years old, there is a newness to the Word because Christ is using it to speak to us again. "There is no historical distance from his word," Hans Urs von Balthasar says.[4] The Word of God is both rooted in the past and, like a two-edged sword, presently cutting through our hearts afresh.

So when we read about Christ addressing the Samaritan woman at the well in John 4, we read about a woman who is alienated from God and her neighbors, sinful, and full of shame. Christ truly did address a woman at a well in Samaria, but as we read the story we, too, are being addressed by Christ. I, too, am in need of what Christ offers to an alienated and sinful soul. I, too, am the dried up soul always "running after the early water every day because I have lost my grasp of the heavenly water I am really seeking."[5]

Christ sat next to this woman as she tried hard to hide her sin and shame. But he saw all the way through her and said, "You are right in saying, 'I have no husband'; for you have had five husbands." And it is the same Christ who sits next to me when I try to hide and act as if I am not full of sin and shame. He sees all the way through me and shows me my sin. He always sees and offers water for healing and refreshment. And when he shows me my sin, I surprisingly feel less alienated, just like the woman, who said to her friends, "Come, see a man who told me all that I ever did" (John 4:29).

We are participants in the text, not mere observers. Remember the story of the centurion who watched Jesus die on the cross in

Mark 15? He was one of the soldiers who had nailed Jesus there. And when Jesus died, the earth shook, the curtain in the temple tore in two from top to bottom, and the skies went dark in the middle of the day. The soldier watched Christ breathe his last breath. "Truly this man was the Son of God!" he says (Mark 15:39). It was the first recorded confession of faith in a crucified Savior. Watching Christ die provoked belief and worship in the Roman soldier. But think of the guilt! He had just crucified the Son of God. He was the one who didn't stop when the whips broke flesh. He was the one who hammered the nails. He was the one gambling for Jesus' clothes. And now, like lights turning on in a dark room, he suddenly sees everything he's done wrong. What hope does he have? The only hope he has is if the Son of God he killed is also the Lamb of God who came to die for his sins.

When we meditate on this story, we are the soldier. It was our sin that caused the death of the Son of God; we are as guilty as the one driving in the nails. What hope do we have? Our only hope is if the Son of God, who we have killed, is also the Lamb of God who came to die for our sins. He split the seas and conquered death so we can walk into the Promised Land. He spilled his blood so that the darkness of death would pass over. He was the firstborn, the only Son, who wouldn't make it through the night, sacrificed so that we might go free as adopted sons and daughters.

Meditating on Scripture can look something like this. First, take a phrase or sentence or truth from the text, something that stuck out to you or warmed your heart. What about this truth is a reason to worship God? How can you adore him? What

attributes of God does it show? Write down anything that
stands out. Tell him what you adore about him. Visualize what
your life, your friends, your church, and your community would
be like if he was adored for this more fully.

Then consider what wrong thoughts, feelings, and behaviors
happen when this truth about God is forgotten. How have you
lived falsely? Confess to him; admit what you've done or who
you are. A simple "Forgive me" can be asked after some reflection. Imagine God responding to your repentance with
words of assurance from Scripture. Visualize what your life
would be like—your decisions, your ambitions—if this truth
was true in your life.

Then reflect on how Jesus is the ultimate revelation of this
attribute. Give thanks for the things he offers for your healing.
Remember his life, or call to mind some story or passage where
this character trait or attribute is displayed. Thank him for who
he is and what he has done.

Finally, ask for the mercy to live more truthfully in the way
of this healing. Ask for help against temptation. Ask for light to
see clearly when you leave this time of prayer and begin the rest
of your day.

You might summarize these steps with adoration, confession,
thanksgiving, and supplication (or asking). I tend to write these
reflections down: What am I adoring? What am I confessing?
What I am thankful for? What do I need? And then I pray the
answers to these questions.

Meditation takes into the midst of God's presence our vulnerable and honest emotional responses to the truth of God's
Word. In Psalm 77 a miracle happens between verses 9 and 13:

there are real doubt and real anger, but joy wins in the end. That's transformation. It may not happen for you every time. Remember, this is a model of prayer, not a formula. You can't produce this miracle—that's God's work. But you can put yourself in the way of the miracle. You can open yourself up for change and make yourself vulnerable to healing.

Maybe you're thinking, *I'm okay. I'm joyful, happy. I don't need this yet.* But there will be a time when the darkness comes. It happens. It's not if but when—a time of suffering, loss, pain, or confusion. And you will need to be able to find your way through the dark.

And meditation is not just for the sorrowful, despairing times. It's for the great days of joy, rehearsing the wonders and glory of God, his work, his salvation, his love—remembering, pondering, and meditating. We meditate on the history of God's right hand now, memorizing the paths of his love, so that when the sorrow comes, we can find our way through the dark.

CHAPTER NINE

SOLITUDE

AFTER CHURCH ONE SUNDAY I asked our youngest daughter what she had learned in class. "That God is in our belly," she said confidently.

"God is where?" I asked, confused.

"God is in *our belly*," she said again, losing none of her previous confidence.

I looked at her older brother and asked, "What did you all learn in class?"

"That for some, their belly is god," he said. For a moment longer I was still confused, and then it clicked. Our church was studying Philippians, where Paul says of those who are enemies of the cross, "their god is their belly" (Philippians 3:19). And although she misheard the exact phrasing, our daughter wasn't confused about the lesson.

Our lives are defined by what we value and love the most. We human beings are driven by what we *want*. We think we know what we love and value the most, but what truly drives us is often a deep mystery. Sam Anderson writes in the *New York Times Magazine*,

> I like to think of myself as an ethical person, but there is almost nothing I wouldn't, in some sense, sell. For instance: There are close family relationships that I have cut off, without even really deciding to, for years at a time. I sold them for stability and mental peace—transactions I think of with doubt and unhappiness every single day. This would seem to suggest that I love my stability and mental peace above all else. And yet I sell those too, at cut-rate prices, again and again: I sell them for the tiny blinking world inside my phone, the anxious grind of tweets and news alerts and emails. We sell what we love best almost every moment of every day. Perhaps we don't really love it. Perhaps we love what we sell it for. Perhaps we are fooling ourselves about what we really value. Perhaps we deserve the modern world.[1]

Maybe we do not know ourselves quite as deeply and fully as we think. The spiritual giants of the past came to realize that those deeper desires, the ones that have a grasp on the inner workings of our hearts, are often hard to understand, uproot, and change. Spiritual habits are rhythms and disciplines aimed at those deeper desires.

One of those disciplines is *solitude*. Solitude isn't talked about much in modern (and especially Western) Christianity, mainly because much of the United States and other Western countries aren't environments where quiet hearts are easily nurtured.

But for Christians throughout history, solitude has been important for understanding questions such as Why am I the way I am? How am I doing? Where is God working in my life and in the world around me? Solitude is gathering ourselves in the presence of God for the purpose of seeing ourselves and our lives from God's perspective. It's the normal rhythm of quietly listening to the voice of God so that when circumstances are not quiet, our hearts are not disquieted.

LEARNING FROM DAVID

The place to begin exploring Christian solitude is Psalm 62 by King David. David begins, "For God alone my soul waits in silence" (v. 1). That's a good start.

God is doing wonderful things all around us that we usually do not stop and see. Annie Dillard writes,

> If the landscape reveals one certainty, it is that the extravagant gesture is the very stuff of creation. After one extravagant gesture of creation in the first place, the universe has continued to deal exclusively in extravagances, flinging intricacies and colossi down aeons of emptiness, heaping profusions on profligacies with ever fresh vigor. The whole show has been on fire from the word go.[2]

God has been dealing in extravagant gestures since the beginning, with beauty and wonder, healing, and grace, whether we see it or not. Right from the beginning of this psalm, David is saying that the least we can do is try to be there. Solitude is the act of trying to *be there*.

In this first verse, David points out the three ingredients for solitude: (1) For God alone (2) my soul waits (3) in silence.

For God alone. Here, at the very beginning, we are stopped short with a surprise. Our solitude is primarily about God, not ourselves. Solitude is not me time or alone time. As important as those things may be, they aren't David's concern. The habit of solitude is for linking up with God in his view of us, ensuring primarily that our lives are centered more on God than on ourselves.

Do you see? Solitude is important because we are prone to do just the opposite. We impulsively make our life about ourselves, which is the beginning of unhappiness. Solitude saves us from our own perspective, encouraging us toward a wider view than we're accustomed to or comfortable with—a view that is not our own. God has a view of the entire landscape, and we need him in order to see reality from beyond our incestuous imaginations. Without him, we get stuck in the loop of our own self-grandeur. "*For God alone* my soul waits in silence."

My soul waits. Waiting is the part of solitude that exposes all our vulnerabilities. No one wants to wait. We want immediate results. And if we can't have immediate results, give us something, *anything*, until we can.

If one of my children acts out, usually he or she has not only disobeyed me but also has frustrated me. What feels good at the moment is to lose my temper and yell, to give a harsh word. What am I doing? I'm giving in to what feels good. I feel better almost immediately. But I know God wants me to parent with gentleness, to be firm but with self-control, to speak in ways that don't crush but build up.

When I do that, it's painful. It does not feel as good, at least not immediately. But in doing so I'm trusting that it will be more satisfying in the end, that God will be honored, and that it's better for my kids' hearts. In a way, that's waiting. I'm waiting for the satisfaction to come on God's terms, not mine.

Waiting is difficult. Instead, we reach for the most fleshy, blinking, beeping, twinkling thing within our reach. We absolutely do not want to wait. We just *want*. Solitude is the intentional and regular habit of waiting.

In silence. Silence is terrifying. We do anything to avoid it. It's awkward to walk through a grocery store with no soundtrack going. Play something—anything! Just don't leave us in silence. We don't want to be left alone with our thoughts. But silence in solitude is not being left alone; it's listening. I've said that prayer is the communion of a loving relationship. A relationship is not one sided, where we do all the talking and God does all the listening. Solitude is the move from being the primary actor in our prayers to receiving whatever God has for us.

To listen in solitude is to let the Word of God act on us. We've taken the truth of the Scripture and pressed into it, and now we're quietly letting the truth press into us.

THE PRACTICE OF SOLITUDE

In my practice, solitude often looks like taking ten or fifteen minutes after I've read and meditated on a passage of Scripture to sit quietly and let the truth of that passage expand in my heart, listening to God speak as my Father through those words.

I set a timer for ten or fifteen minutes (I don't want to have to keep looking at the clock), close my Bible and my journal, and invite God to speak, to be present, to show me what he sees.

> Search me, O God, and know my heart!
>   Try me and know my thoughts!
> And see if there be any grievous way in me,
>   and lead me in the way everlasting! (Psalm 139:23-24)

I often start my time by quoting Psalm 62:1, "For you alone, my soul waits in silence." In previous chapters I've described a way of praying or meditating that imagines what God might say to us as our Father, what Christ might say as our Brother and Savior, what the Spirit might say as our Counselor or Comforter. That's a very intimate way of reading Scripture and hearing God's Word. But solitude is waiting to hear how God comforts and heals apart from our own imagination.

And God does work in us. Sometimes it's sensing God's presence more clearly or maturing in our trust in him. Other times it's God pressing into our consciousness a truth about ourselves we had not seen before, showing us a fuller picture of ourselves. Maybe a hurting friend is brought to mind, and we are led to pray for them. What happens can be dramatic, but often it's what the prophet Elijah experienced as a "still small voice" (1 Kings 19:12 KJV). Nevertheless, St. Bernard encourages us, "God is never sought in vain, even when he cannot be found."[3] Or as John Owen puts it, "He will never be as water that fails, nor has he at any time said to his people, 'Seek my face in vain.'"[4]

In these times I've found pleasure, insight, love, and comfort. There have been times when I've felt a great weight so heavy upon me that sitting in my chair I cannot move, nor do I want to. There have also been many times of boredom and distraction when I come expecting intimate solitude and the next thing I know, I'm thinking about something else, some worry or conflict, some task ahead, and I feel as if I've wasted the time. In those moments I cast those cares on him and remind myself that God is gracious, and I merely redirect my thoughts to him again—no need for condemnation now, just focus.

In a letter to a little girl in 1950, C. S. Lewis says this about feelings in our spiritual practices,

> Don't expect (I mean, don't count on and don't demand) . . . you will have all the feelings you would like to have. You may, of course: but also you may not. But don't worry if you don't get them. They aren't what matter. The things that are happening to you are quite real things whether you feel as you would wish or not, just as a meal will do a hungry person good even if he has a cold in the head which will rather spoil the taste. Our Lord will give us right feelings if he wishes— and then we must say Thank you. If he doesn't, then we must say to ourselves (and to Him) that he knows best.[5]

About once a month I'll meditate on a psalm and take a bit longer in silence, maybe twenty to thirty minutes. It's challenging, and you may need to work up to it. I did. In that silence my intention is to pay attention to every worry and anxiety that surfaces. I write them down and ask God to help and heal. It's how I cast my cares on him.

Here's another way to practice solitude: at the end of the day, put your phone aside and take a moment to pay attention to what

God did today. What can you give thanks for? Where did peace reign? Where did you experience grace? Consider how you responded to conflict, fear, or worry. Then repent of the things you need to, and give thanks for the times when God provided victory. Christians have traditionally called this the "daily examen."

These practices of solitude can look different. They can be restful or times of great struggle. It depends on the person and what kind of season he or she is in. But the characteristics of fruitful solitude are regularity, stillness, and listening. Would you characterize your spiritual life with any of these?

THE NEED FOR SOLITUDE

Solitude settles us into God's universe, not ours. It provides a true perspective of ourselves and God. To practice solitude is to obey the command of Psalm 46:10 (emphasis added): "*Be still,* and know that I am God." We can't nurture the truth of God's lordship in our lives while in a hurry. In a hurry, we depend more on our human impulses and instincts, which naturally make us lords over our own lives. But that is spiritual disaster.

In Psalm 62:3 David complains that his enemies are after him. He says that he feels like a "leaning wall, a tottering fence." He's not doing well emotionally. Most of us don't see the seriousness of our condition until we collapse in crisis. Once we get to level ten, we can see that we're a mess, but what about levels two or three? Solitude reveals how the pressures of life are affecting us long before we collapse, and it guards us against experiencing pain or causing pain to others.

Psychologist Jonathan Smallwood has produced research showing that a wandering mind and boredom are important for what he calls "autobiographical planning," giving us a greater ability to assess how we are doing and where we are going.[6]

If letting our minds wander is important for emotional health, how much more is solitude with God important for our spiritual health? In solitude, not only our conscious and subconscious lives are making a connection, but we are also connecting with God himself, who can see into the depths of our hearts and can reveal the narrative arc of our lives and how it relates to his narrative arc.

Solitude gives us the perspective we need to live truthfully in this world. Psalm 62:9 confesses a reality that we often distort: the lowliest people in this world may be but a breath, but those who are of high estate are deluding themselves. "They are together lighter than a breath." The psalmist is talking about weightiness: the *weightiest* people on earth are but a breath compared to God.

We are constantly seeking glory from others. We long to be praised and adored, and we're willing to sacrifice so much to be loved. But the psalmist is pressing into the reality that if all the world loved us, it would still be just a breath compared to the weightiness of the love and affirmation of God. If we don't take time for solitude, humans will seem weighty, and God will seem inconsequential and light. But God is not, and the freest and happiest people in the world know it.

A SOLITUDE OF THE HEART

In Psalm 62 David is not just aiming for a quiet heart. David is the ruler of a young nation and is frequently on the run from enemies. He doesn't live a quiet life in a quiet place. "But the solitude that really counts," says Henri Nouwen, "is the solitude of the heart; it is an inner quality or attitude that does not depend on physical isolation. On occasion the isolation is necessary to develop a solitude of the heart." This mindset, he says, can be "maintained and developed in the center of a big city, in the middle of a large crowd, and in the context of a very active and productive life."[7]

Solitude is not only for those who are temperamentally relaxed or contemplative or who can escape from the big city to the mountains of Montana to find true solitude. It's not true. You can be a busy, productive executive, a mother of young children, or a student in a competitive school and still have a quiet heart. In fact, people who maintain regular times of solitude with God are some of the most fruitful and productive people I know. They know when to take risks because they have a better perspective on themselves and God. They not only think straight, they feel straight too.

David is looking for God with a quiet heart in a world that does not often offer quiet circumstances. Solitude is the discipline of continually coming to God to form an inner stillness so that when circumstances are not quiet, our hearts are not shaken. We've learned where our fortress is, how the balances come out, what is weighty in this world, and what is just a breath.

HINDRANCES TO SOLITUDE

If solitude is deep work, it shouldn't surprise us when we meet resistance. No one is a natural at Christian solitude. Deep work is slow work, with successes and failures along the way. I find it a great comfort that David found it difficult too: "For God alone my soul waits in silence." He states it as a fact. It's what he does.

Then four verses later, his tone changes, "For God alone, O my soul, wait in silence" (Psalm 62:5). Did you catch the difference? Verse 1 states a fact about his soul; verse 5 commands his soul to get in line with what he knows to be true. He's arguing with himself. *This is what you must do! You wait for him, alone!* But it's not natural for him. He must preach to himself.

Being still is hard because that's when our anxieties, fears, loneliness, and insecurities come to the surface. In *Reclaiming Conversation*, Sherry Turkle, a researcher at MIT, says that "research shows that people are uncomfortable if left alone with their thoughts, even for a few minutes."[8] I wonder if you resonate with this claim. Maybe you think, *That's not me!* If you don't believe Turkle, consider what happens when we stand in a long line at a coffee shop or when we're waiting for a bus—what do we reach for? Our phone? *I've got to do something. It's just a time filler. It doesn't say anything deep about me.* Maybe—but how anxious do you get when you accidently leave your phone behind? *That never happens!* Okay, how are your anxiety levels when you're leaving the house and you see your battery is at 4 percent? How freaked out do you get? We don't want to be alone.

Turkle continues, "These results are stunning, but in a way, not surprising. These days, we see that when people are alone at a stop sign or in the checkout line at the supermarket, they seem almost panicked and they reach for their phones. We are so accustomed to being always connected that being alone seems like a problem technology should solve."[9]

When we spend time in solitude, we will feel the desert feelings of loneliness. We can sense all the insecurities and vulnerabilities. Things come to the surface that we've become very good at pushing down over the years. Nouwen says that one of the basic steps of Christian maturity is growing out of those desert feelings of loneliness and boredom and into the garden of solitude and stillness.[10] Solitude is the rhythm of coming to God in stillness with our insecurities and loneliness and learning to experience more of the presence, companionship, and communion of God.

Thanks to our devices, we never have to feel the pain of being alone. Nir Eyal writes, "Feelings of boredom, loneliness, frustration, confusion, and indecisiveness often instigate a slight pain or irritation and prompt an almost instantaneous and often mindless action to quell the negative sensation."[11] Social media relieves, in small measures, the apprehension of loneliness and numbs our fears with little status updates, getting likes, retweets, and replies. Each time, our brain gets a little hit of dopamine, leaving us craving another hit. It's a reward system. That's why Alexis Madrigal says that people look at their social media feeds without "even clicking the links or responding to people. I'm just scrolling down, or worse, pulling with my thumb, reloading, reloading." Why? Because our brains are wired for habits, and the scrolling, pulling down with the thumb, and double tapping bring a reward that our brains have learned to crave.

Madrigal calls it the "machine zone."

What is the machine zone? It's a rhythm. It's a response to a fine-tuned feedback loop. It's a powerful space-time distortion. You hit a button. Something happens. You hit it again. Something similar, but not exactly the same happens. Maybe you win, maybe you don't. Repeat. Repeat. Repeat. Repeat. Repeat. It's the pleasure of the repeat, the security of the loop.

Like slot machines, our devices "exploit the human desire for flow, but without the meaning or mastery attached to the state."[12]

This "human desire for flow" is our human desire for rhythm, which is most beneficial when it shapes our inner life toward something greater than itself—like rhythms of exercise for the purpose of bodily health or rhythms of worship for spiritual health. When we exercise, we master our lethargy; when we worship, we master our sin. Healthy rhythms, physically and spiritually, provide meaning.

Our phones sync us to a rhythm by which we're mastered by something less than meaningful. They deplete our inner life rather than building it up. They trick us into thinking we're living moments of *more*, but really we are living lives of *less*. This is what Madrigal calls "the dark side of the 'flow.'" No wonder frequent social media use has been linked to feelings of depression and social anxiety.[13]

Busy, ambitious people take in an overload of information. When we have lots of information input, the area of our brains that makes intentional choices becomes less active and the part that drives us by habits and learned behavior takes the wheel. As a result, many of our decisions are made by habit. After a long day of overstimulation, we fall back on our habits—and for many of us that means social media. While we may read Twitter and Facebook in the morning, following links and engaging with individuals, at night we scroll mindlessly.[14]

There is one further dark side of this: when we get tired, it's not just the intentional decision-making parts of our brains that are tired but also the moral parts. So habits take over, and we use the internet mindlessly. The danger is that the reward of scrolling and refreshing easily transfers to the rewards of porn or other destructive online behaviors. Habits that cause depletion rather than life and health (emotionally and spiritually) always have a downward spiral. In other words, when we're tired after a full day of information overload, we don't engage the material we encounter online with the wisdom we might have had earlier in the day. We might type out angry comments on social media, indulge in images we shouldn't look at, mindlessly follow link after link, or purchase things we normally wouldn't.

Heavy social media use makes solitude with God scattered and frustrating. But healthy rhythms of solitude and even boredom, supported by resistance to technology (maybe through intentional times of disconnecting from social media), can bring surprising richness and refreshment to our lives. Take a week (or a month!) off social media on a regular basis, and turn off your phone when you come home. Use an analog clock for an alarm instead of your phone. Practice being quiet or paying attention to a book, a friend, or God for longer segments of time than you're normally comfortable doing.

FRUIT OF SOLITUDE

In Psalm 62:8 David turns to the community of faith and says,

> Trust in him at all times, O people;
>> pour out your heart before him;
>> God is a refuge for us.

David has now turned from his still, listening moment to encourage others.

Solitude doesn't drive us deeper into ourselves but out toward others. Thomas Merton wrote, "If you go into the desert merely to get away from people you dislike, you will find neither peace nor solitude; you will only isolate yourself with a tribe of devils."[15] Solitude develops our inner lives to love what God loves—and God loves our neighbors.

There is a circle of virtue in solitude. In it we consider ourselves truthfully in God's presence. He shows us who we are and who he is and gives us a sense of security. In solitude we do not merely "find ourselves,"—we find ourselves in Christ. When we find ourselves in Christ, we don't have to search for security from or in others. We don't have to use human relationships to find what we can only find fully in Christ. We are free to love and listen and serve others out of that security.

The circle of virtue in solitude, then, looks like this: (1) we consider ourselves deeply in the presence of Christ, and in doing so (2) we find ourselves securely in Christ, which leads us to (3) discovering resources and power to love those whom Christ loves. But to sustain that behavior of loving those Christ loves, (4) we are driven back to solitude to the infinite well of divine resources.

So we have made a surprising discovery. The best way to love and care for those in our community is to regularly practice solitude with God.

Solitude provides a way to seek others, not in order to get something but simply because I love them. In this way I can experience the kind of intimacy with others that God uses to heal and restore. I can gain deeper friendships, and my friends become the deeper means by which God ministers to me and to them.

Solomon says, "A gentle tongue is a tree of life" (Proverbs 15:4). A tree of life is a source of healing and renewal. Solitude provides a way of becoming like a tree of life, with roots down deep in a source of healing. We've experienced that healing in such a profound way that the very fruit of our lives with God is healing words: words that restore, that make others feel safe and more at home. Something profound must happen within us to become like that. Solitude is the pathway toward it.

CHAPTER TEN

FASTING AND FEASTING

IN *THE SUPPER OF THE LAMB*, Robert Capon imagines a fictional scenario at a dinner party:

"What can I give you, Harry? Large helping or small?"

"If it's all the same to you, Martha, just a little of the Chicken Paprikash. No noodles. I'm counting calories."

In this scenario Martha has made noodles from scratch—something that Harry will not likely have before him again in years—but he turns them down because "it is calories, not the noodles, that count." What is grievous to Capon is that a calorie "is not a thing; it is a measurement." Calories can't be smelled, savored, or eaten. Martha has labored over real food, but all Harry sees is an abstraction.[1]

We can have sympathy for Harry. He is likely responding to a history of overeating and lack of self-control, and now he's trying to kill his food idol the way his culture teaches him. To be honest, I often count calories myself. After my midthirties, my "metabolic rate," as Capon says, "retired from the rat race and settled down to a truly dignified and leisurely pace."[2] I remember hurting my back just by pushing down the trash in its can to make more space. *Pinch*, I was on the floor. I called my dad, who has had back problems in the past. He told me, very subtly, "It sounds like the front of your body is too heavy for the back." Right, ho!

I took measures. I changed my exercise habits and my diet. Both were hard changes. More regular exercise meant I had to take time away from other important things, and changing my diet meant resisting wonderfully tasty things. "Cutting back" on calories, however, didn't make a significant dent in my weight. My body seemed to be on a trajectory of growth fueled by a kind of momentum and determination that mere calorie counting could not much disturb. The final stab in my heart—or tummy— came in my favorite Hungarian pastry shop, where I enjoyed reading or working with coffee and a slice of baklava. Baklava is a pastry made with phyllo, a very thin unleavened dough, stretched into paper-thin sheets, anointed with olive oil and butter, baked with nuts, and sweetened with honey. It is manna handed down from the Ottoman Empire.

Baklava's ingredients were joy—but joy had too many calories. When I realized it, I saw then and there that I could not carry on this relationship with food. I had mistaken what the true dilemma was. I thought I had to choose either enjoying food with declining health, or consuming mediocre meals coupled with a healthy body.

But I didn't have to give up on enjoyment. I just had to choose to take enjoyment more seriously. "A man who takes a small helping," says Capon, "is a man without eyes to see what is in front of him. Accordingly, I passed back for seconds and then thirds, and made a vow then and there to walk more, to split logs every day and above all, to change my religion from the devilish cult of dieting to the godly discipline of fasting. . . . If I ate, I would eat without stint; and if I stinted, I would not eat at all."[3]

Religious people, Christians included, have a tendency to emphasize discipline over joy, so we talk of fasting without feasting. But the Bible entices its readers with visions of feasts and suppers more than instructions about fasting. Fasts in the Bible are not ends unto themselves. They are the means.

If my wife said to me, "I'm going to prepare a feast tonight. I am making a balsamic seared lamb," I ought to plan my day accordingly, in preparation for the evening feast. But what if, instead, I start off by eating a huge breakfast: bacon, eggs, and waffles. Then I have a 10 a.m. meeting, where I have coffee and a snack. At a lunch meeting I have baked ziti with a side order of garlic bread. On my way home I stop at a deli and pick up a Snickers bar, since I have some afternoon hunger pangs. Then I get home and dinner is ready. The feast is prepared. My wife has made the lamb that's paired beautifully with Dijon glazed carrots and roasted butternut squash with garlic and parsley, and dessert is coming.

But I'm not hungry. In fact, the wonderful dinner doesn't even entice me.

What should have happened? I should have eaten toast for breakfast and salad for lunch, and endured the afternoon hunger pangs so when the feast came, I was ready for it.

When someone prepares you a feast, you do not want to be full, nor do you want to be counting calories. "Let him fast until he is free to eat like a true son of Adam," says Capon. "I would rather have one magnificent feast followed by a day of no meals at all than two days full of mediocre meals at close intervals. Modern people constantly have immediate mediocre food at their fingertips so we have no idea what it means to prepare to feast—we just go along in life just sort of full and never fully satisfied."[4]

For modern people, fasting can mean something like a protest fast, like Mahatma Gandhi fasting in protest of the British rule in India. Gandhi, along with the others who joined him, decided not to eat until things changed. It was an act of asserting themselves. Or perhaps when we hear of fasting we think of the intermittent fasting we sometimes do to lose weight—another form of self-assertion.

But biblical fasting is different. It's not a way of asserting what we need or want. It is a way to open ourselves up to the presence of God.

> The real secret of fasting is not that it is a simple way to keep one's weight down, but it is a mysterious way of lifting creation into the Supper of the Lamb. It is not a little excursion into fashionable shape, but a major entrance into the fasting, the agony, the passion by which the Incarnate Word restores all things to the goodness God finds in them. It is as much an act of prayer as prayer itself, and in an affluent society, it may well be the most meaningful of all the practices of religion—the most likely point at which the salt can find its savor again.[5]

Fasting is for feasting. But not just for earthly feasts—fasting opens us up to a deeper hunger that mediocre meals often numb us to. Fasting is the spiritual exercise of preparing and sustaining our appetite for God.

Our prayers are enhanced by fasting since it grows our hunger for God over other things we ordinarily crave. Prayer and communion with God become like feasts, satisfying our hunger that can only come from being with God. The devil tempted Jesus in the wilderness, saying, "Command these stones to become loaves of bread." Jesus was certainly hungry after fasting forty days in the wilderness, but in his fasting a deeper hunger had risen to the surface. "Man shall not live by bread alone, but by every word that comes from the mouth of God," Jesus said (Matthew 4:3-4).

The regular rhythm of fasting guards against spiritual lethargy. If we struggle with the desire for prayer, the discipline of fasting helps us along the way.

> When you fast, do not look gloomy like the hypocrites, for they disfigure their faces that their fasting may be seen by others. Truly, I say to you, they have received their reward. But when you fast, anoint your head and wash your face, that your fasting may not be seen by others but by your Father who is in secret. And your Father who sees in secret will reward you. (Matthew 6:16-18)

This passage teaches us that there's a way to practice fasting that spoils its purpose and thus squanders the joy. There's another way to fast that enhances its joy.

The way to spoil the purpose of fasting is to practice it where others can see. This is true of all spiritual practices, whether prayer, giving, or fasting. When we practice spiritual habits where others can see and think well of us, what people think of us will be our reward, Jesus says. Being well thought of by others may seem nice, but there is a much better reward available.

In fact, Jesus calls this behavior hypocrisy. He is talking about people who always find a way to talk about how disciplined they are and how much time they spend in prayer—not to edify others but to be considered great.

It's likely we all know the obnoxious behavior of those who make a show of their religious enthusiasm. But Jesus takes on an even more dangerous sort. He is addressing those who know how to both be seen and appear humble. These people aren't completely unaware of what they're doing, though they may be asleep to much of it. They've developed their pride in a way that looks like humility. They fast and look gloomy and exhausted. "You okay?" someone asks. "Oh, yeah," they say, "thanks for asking. I'm just fasting."

Instead, Jesus says, when you fast, anoint your head and wash your face. *Face* is important in biblical imagery because the face is an indication of what's going on inside the person. It's a peek into the inner life. You can often tell what someone is thinking or feeling by his or her face. So if you want to fool someone about what's going on inside, intentionally make your face different. If you're sad, you put on a smiling face; if you're fearful, you put on a bold face. The face communicates what's going on inside.

So consider what Jesus is asking his listeners to do. When we fast, we are cutting ourselves off from normal comforts and pleasures so we can experience ultimate comforts and pleasures from God. If we're fasting, then, a disfigured and sad face probably fits what's going on inside. But Jesus is saying, when you fast, wash your face and anoint your head with oil—make yourself look good.

This can be confusing at first. It seems as if Jesus is instructing his listeners to be misleading when they fast. "You will feel miserable, but I want you to act and behave as if you're not."

Jesus is teaching us a principle that's important for not only fasting but for all spiritual disciplines: spiritual disciplines aren't meant to be displayed for other people, who can merely see the face. They're meant for the One who can see the heart. Fasting is ultimately for God.

The hypocrisy Jesus is referring to is not that something inside our life is different from the outside, but that we're pretending to be fasting for God when really we're fasting for others. When we do that, Jesus says, we have our reward already.

But Jesus points to a deeper spiritual principle. He tells us to wash our face and anoint ourselves when we are fasting. Interestingly, these are things people in Jesus' day would do when they prepared to eat. Jesus isn't just saying we shouldn't show our fasting to others; he's saying we ought to go out of our way to resist the praise of others.

The message is clear for those of us who know how to look humble and still receive praise. The longer we are Christians, the easier this form of spiritual pride becomes. We learn what words to use. We learn how to put ourselves in the way of praise without looking obnoxious. Often we do it unconsciously. Thomas Merton says,

Here is a man who has done many things that were hard for his flesh to accept. He has come through difficult trials and done a lot of work, and by God's grace he has come to possess a habit of fortitude and self-sacrifice in which, at last, labor and suffering become easy. It is reasonable that his conscience should be at peace. But before he realizes it, the clean peace of a will united to God becomes the complacency of a will that loves its own excellence.[6]

The pleasure of being seen and admired consumes all the joys of this person's reward with God. "The warmth of that fire" that he feels in the admiration of others, "feels very much like the love of God. . . . He burns with self-admiration and thinks: 'It is the fire of the love of God.'"[7]

We learn, almost intuitively, how to seek praise without looking insufferable. But do we know how to resist it and keep a hidden, quiet heart? Jesus is describing a fast inside a fast: on the one hand, we're fasting from food, learning to sustain our appetite for God; but we're also fasting from the glory and praise of others, since it's likely we crave it more than we're fully aware. There is a crucifying power of doing things for God in hiddenness and secret. Intentionally resisting praise expands and grows our heart for Christ.

When we think about rewards, we often think of *getting what we deserve*. We work in such a way to get a reward that corresponds to our effort.

But the reward Jesus is referring to is not meritorious. Fasting does not put God in our debt. It is not a technique that puts us in good standing with God. God offers, as a gift, the satisfaction of our desires—desires that are ultimately for him.

David explains this reward further in Psalm 63. He begins the psalm by saying to the Lord,

> O God, you are my God; earnestly I seek you;
>> my soul thirsts for you;
> my flesh faints for you,
>> as in a dry and weary land where there is no water. (v. 1)

David has developed a hunger, an appetite for God. He goes on,

> So I have looked upon you in the sanctuary,
>> beholding your power and glory.
> Because your steadfast love is better than life. (vv. 2-3)

Notice all the action verbs? *Seek* you; *thirst* for you; *faint* for you; *look* to you; *behold* you. Is that characteristic of your spiritual life? Is there seeking, thirsting, fainting, looking, beholding?

Then David describes the reward of all these actions:

> My soul will be satisfied as with fat and rich food,
>> and my mouth will praise you with joyful lips. (v. 5)

He's describing the satisfaction of eating a rich and satisfying feast. God has prepared a feast for David. What makes it a feast is that he hasn't gone after the easy comfort of mediocre meals. He has learned how to be hungry.

All of us keep things in our lives that dampen our hunger for God, so we never feel the deep hunger pangs of our souls. We are always full but never satisfied. Regular rhythms of fasting have a way of connecting our physical hunger to our spiritual hunger. The growl of our stomachs reminds us that we also have a growl in our souls. We can fast from all kinds of things—

media, alcohol, chocolate—but there's something about physical hunger that transforms our hearts.

As in other spiritual disciplines, there's an element of waiting in fasting. It teaches our hearts that we need something deeper than bread and more sustaining than water. Paul says in 1 Corinthians 6:13, "'Food is meant for the stomach and the stomach for food,' and God will destroy both." He's quoting a popular saying among the first-century Corinthians, which implies that our sexual desires are as natural as our cravings for food. Just as we eat when we're hungry, so we have sex when we crave it. It's as simple as that.

But Paul argues that our desires are not primarily meant for immediate gratification. Our bodies and our desires find their ultimate fulfillment in God. "Do you not know that your bodies are members of Christ? . . . Do you not know that your body is a temple of the Holy Spirit within you, whom you have from God? You are not your own, for you were bought with a price" (1 Corinthians 6:15, 19-20).

Fasting, then, teaches our hearts that satisfaction in God, rather than immediate gratification in food (or sex or social media), makes us more joyful in this world. Fasting enlarges our hearts and deepens our joy in God by making more room for him rather than cluttering our hearts up with mediocre things.

Fasts lead to feasts. If fasting lifts creation up to the Supper of the Lamb, feasting gives us a taste of it. We ought to grow our hunger for God, but let's not pretend God is stingy—he owns the cattle on a thousand hills. Earthly feasts prepare us for heavenly ones, giving testimony to what they will be like. "Man invented cooking," says Capon, "before he thought of nutrition.

To be sure, food keeps us alive but that is only its small and most temporary work. Its eternal purpose is to furnish our sensibilities against the day when we shall sit down at the heavenly banquet and see how gracious the Lord is." Fasts teach us how to be hungry; feasts teach us how to be full. Both teach us about heaven and how to be satisfied when we get there. "Nourishment is necessary only for a while; what we shall need forever is taste."[8]

So, yes, we ought to practice a regular rhythm of fasting but stabilize our souls with feasts too. If you've never practiced either on a regular basis, let me offer some guidance.

A traditional time when Christians ordinarily take time to fast is Lent, right before Easter. Or you may be facing a season of spiritual dryness or distance from God and long for more intimacy. So make space in your week for fasting. Start with a meal. Make some accommodations ahead of time to fast in private. If you are at work during your times of fasting, have some plans on how to keep your fasts for God to see rather than others. During lunch, instead of eating, use the time to pray.

Jesus says in the wilderness while he's fasting, "Man shall not live by bread alone, but by every word that comes from the mouth of God" (Matthew 4:4). God's Word is more necessary to us than bread. So when you fast, do what is more necessary. Take the time you would've spent eating and meditate on Scripture. Pray for others, confess sin, and enjoy God's Word, even while you're feeling the pangs of hunger.

Let your hunger pangs remind you of Christ's hunger in the wilderness. The Spirit who led Jesus into the wilderness (Matthew 4:1) is the same Spirit who sustains you in your own hunger. Remind yourself of Christ's thirst on the cross (John 19:28)—

when the soldiers heard him cry out they gave him a sponge full of sour, bitter wine. Remember that because of our sin, we deserve that sour, bitter drink with its wrath and condemnation. But Christ, the perfect Son, drank the bitterness for us. He cried out for God and dreamed about the feast—"My soul will be satisfied as with fat and rich food." Jesus had experienced that feast with the Father from all eternity. Now he experienced thirst and hunger. But because he thirsted, our thirst can be quenched; because he went hungry, our hunger is satisfied.

Perhaps most challenging is not the time during your usual meal when you pray but the time after. Your body wants relief. A simple prayer—"Help me, Father," "Give me strength, Lord," "Satisfy me with your presence, Christ"—will suffice. Trust that the Lord will supply what you need. If you fail, don't be hard on yourself. Try again the next week and pray for help during the week as the day arrives. Remember, fasting doesn't merit anything. It doesn't get us into the feast—Jesus does. But fasting does stir and excite the taste buds of our hearts for the true feast of Christ. As you go about your daily labors while you experience hunger, remember that Christ is with you while you work and that every work, however large or small, is done for Christ's glory.

As you can, increase your fasting to two meals or to a whole day. As with any discipline, it's best to progress incrementally. The amount of time is not the point; the goal is to increasingly stir your hunger and dependence on Christ, exposing some things (like food or drink) that have control over you. Remember that being disciplined is not sanctification in itself. You may be able to fast seven days and still be filled with pride. Seek humility, letting your fasts constantly lead you to neediness and hunger for the Lord. The fruit of your fasts should be more thanksgiving, more awareness of personal sin, and softness of heart. Be wary if your fasts lead to self-righteousness or grumbling.

Longer fasts should be undertaken with some counsel, and not just a doctor's. Multiday fasts can bring spiritual breakthroughs, but they should be done carefully, with some direction from a pastor or mentor about why or how a longer fast should be undertaken and with wisdom on what to expect.

There are different reasons in Scripture to fast: in response to personal sin (Joel 2:12-13), in times of great urgency of need (Esther 9:30-31), to increase humility (Ezra 8:21), to grieve (Judges 20:26; 1 Samuel 31:13), as an expression of worship (Acts 13:2), and others. But at the core, fasting should stir our inner hunger for God.

Fasts should be followed by feasts. If you are coming off a day-long or multiday fast, a large multicourse meal may not be easy on your intestines, so give yourself space. Maybe break your fast with a smoothie and then feast the next day. But feast we should, and we should do it in good company.

Gather friends for a meal that everyone is involved in making. Come prepared. Take a nap or sleep longer the night before—no one goes home early from a good feast. Feasts are eternal reminders that food "will always be more delicious than it is useful."[9] So pay attention to calories and nutrition during other times in the week so you won't have to at the feast.

Set aside phones at the door. Email, text, and Twitter can wait until later. Be present with the people you're with, who brought the food and drink. Maybe try journaling about your feast rather than posting a picture of it on Instagram.

If you're hosting or in charge of the feast, come with fun, engaging topics of discussion that reach beyond superficial gossip. Try every kind of food that's brought and have more than one kind of dessert.

Wine should be served at dinner; have enough available for a few glasses each. Keep the harder liquor for after the meal, when deeper discussions are broken up among smaller groups, scattered around the house.

Have music prepared. A list of songs or a stack of records should be more than just a filler of empty space, but it shouldn't distract from conversation. I've hosted nights when everyone brought a vinyl record of their choice.

Take opportunities to share gratitude, honor one another, give toasts, and even sing if it feels natural. And most of all, remember that Christ is present. Remember he brings the best wine when he comes. He reclines with us, his friends. He's in our stories, he's in our laughter, and he's in our eating and drinking. Those times are best when he is remembered and cherished.

One evening, my wife and I were cleaning up after a meal with friends. As we were rinsing dishes and picking up glasses around the apartment, we laughed together as we remembered some of the best moments of the night. We had been surprised when a shyer friend broke out of her shell and shared her gift of impressions. We were glad to toast to a friend who got his dream job that we'd all been praying for. We were so happy to see a friend who had been distant from us for a while but that night was laughing and seemed to experience love. We were tired and needed to go to bed, but we had full bellies and full hearts—a lot to be thankful for.

The rhythm of feasting and fasting forms hearts at rest with God rather than hearts that restlessly crave the things of this world. It makes the life of prayer easier. Fasting teaches my heart to hunger for the deep things of God. Prayer is the daily feast on those things.

CHAPTER ELEVEN

SABBATH RESTING

AFTER A SUNDAY SERVICE I was sitting with a woman who'd been attending our church for a few months. She had her Bible open and was trying to find a particular passage. She was in her sixties, and this was her first meaningful church experience. Most Sundays she had been frustrated about something I'd said in my sermon, or she had found something confusing. But today was different. She had something she wanted to show me.

"Here," she said. "I found it." And she began to read Jesus' words to me. "Come to me, all you who are weary and burdened, and I will give you rest. Take my yoke upon you and learn from me, for I am gentle and humble in heart, and you will find rest for your souls" (Matthew 11:28-29 NIV).

I had encouraged her to begin reading the Bible for herself and to begin with Matthew or Mark. She began with Matthew and was generally confused most of the time. But she read a chapter or two a day nonetheless. When she came to Matthew 11, she was hit over the head with verse 29: "Take my yoke upon you and learn from me, for I am gentle and humble in heart, and you will find rest for your souls."

"That sounds so wonderful," she said. "And I think I felt it when I read this. I felt a warmth like Jesus was inviting me to rest." She was weary. She put up a strong front, but she was brittle on the inside after years of trials and trouble. The words of Christ felt like a warm blanket to her. They were healing words. They were words of life. For the first time she had found rest, not merely for her body but for her soul.

What my friend experienced at that moment was a Sabbath rest of the heart. She felt peace, healing, restoration, and hope. Maybe you've experienced that too. I hope so. But for many of us, maybe there was a moment of that rest, but it's been a long time since.

When Christ invites us to this rest, he isn't referring to a singular moment or occasional experience but a new kind of life—a new rest of the soul, a sustained kind of rest. Sure, there may be heightened times of peace and satisfaction along with anxious circumstances, but Christ's rest is for us now.

A life of prayer (of communion, meditation, and solitude) is the rhythm that puts us in the pathway of rest. But the weekly discipline of Sabbath rest is a supportive rhythm that solidifies a spirit of rest. We don't often think of rest as a discipline. In fact, my guess is that even Christians who know their Bibles see a day of rest or Sabbath as a day designed primarily for *recovery from* or a *precaution against* exhaustion. The first-century Jewish philosopher Philo of Alexandria once defended the Sabbath, saying,

On this day we are commanded to abstain from all work, not because the law inculcates slackness. . . . Its object is rather to give man relaxation from continuous and unending toil and by refreshing their bodies with a regularly calculated system of remissions to send them out renewed to their old activities. For a breathing spell enables not merely ordinary people but athletes also to collect their strength with a stronger force behind them to undertake promptly and patiently each of the tasks set before them.[1]

Many of us read Philo's description and see the wisdom in this kind of resting—rest actually helps us recover and be more effective in the long run. But what Philo describes here as the Sabbath is not the picture the Bible gives us. For Philo—and for many of us—rest is for the sake of more activity. Its purpose is to make better use of our energy toward more productivity, more efficiency. This mindset can actually discourage rest because if we have enough ambition or fear that can provide enough adrenaline rushing through us, we'll never feel exhausted—at least not for a while.

The Sabbath was made for more than just recovery or preventing exhaustion. It's more than just a way to focus our energy toward more productivity. "The Sabbath," says Abraham Heschel, "is a day for the sake of life. Man is not a beast of burden, and the Sabbath is not for the purpose of enhancing the efficiency of his work."[2] I want to suggest a different way to think about Sabbath rest. The Sabbath is God's weekly invitation to experience a sustaining spiritual vibrancy that many Christians, for one reason or another, have refused to accept. My hope is that you won't.

"If there's one thing we know about everyday life," writes Judith Shulevitz in her book *A Sabbath World*, "it's that we don't have enough time to finish our work and get our chores done and be with family and friends."[3] The things we want to do—that we *should* do—we leave undone or do them poorly. These are often the very things that give our lives meaning, and we're anxious or unhappy when they get sidelined by clutter and busyness.

Yet according to Shulevitz, we do not work more than we used to; we only think we do.

> In 1991, the economist Juliet Schor advanced the now conventional thesis that global competition forced Americans to toil longer and rest less. She based this on rough estimates that people gave during interviews with U.S. census takers over three decades. Meanwhile, two sociologists, John P. Robinson and Geoffrey Godbey, were asking people to fill out time diaries noting exactly how much time they spent on each activity of the day right after they'd done it. They concluded that Americans work less than they did in the 1960s. How do you reconcile what people said with what their time diaries showed? You acknowledge that Americans feel more pressed for time, whether they're working harder or not.[4]

Today, Americans actually work fewer hours than in previous decades, but we feel more pressed for time. Why? What's happened? There are a few theories. One is that increased connectivity often allows us to do our work anywhere. And since we can do our work anywhere, we do our work everywhere. We can work from home, the coffee shop, or on the train. As Shulevitz says, "The irregular work hours nonetheless upset their psychological equilibrium. With a moment snatched here and there, it's hard to achieve that feeling of being in the swing of something, the self-forgetfulness that psychologists call flow."[5] In other words, despite the flexibility technology affords, we're not as productive or efficient as we think, and we have the nagging sense that we're always behind.

Another theory is based on the fact that those same studies show we use the majority of our free time on media use. We spend less time in newspapers or books and more on social media, computer games, and television, which leaves an inordinate amount of pressure on the remaining time to create meaning and to do what makes us happy. This leads to frustration, anxiety, and feelings of apathy.

One other theory is that while we're inundated with products that are meant to save time and make us feel less rushed, the opposite has actually happened. Now, "there are ever more products to consume."[6] These time-saving products, it turns out, take time to consume.

So we have more flexibility at work than we've ever had, more technology to make us more efficient, more products to consume, and even the *feeling* that we're doing more. But under the hood of our inner lives, we don't feel as if we're doing anything meaningful. We always think we're not doing enough, and we never have enough time for all the things we need to do. Who can deliver us?

Shulevitz writes that on the traditional Sabbath "not only did drudgery give way to festivity, family gatherings and occasionally worship, but the machinery of self-censorship shut down, too, stilling the eternal inner murmur of self-reproach."[7]

"The eternal inner murmur of self-reproach." Do you know what she means by that phrase? There's something deep down inside me, an inner murmur, telling me I need to prove myself. Most of us sense that "inner reproach" on our days off: *What I have done is not enough. It's not good enough.* So our days off are not restful but anxious. *I need to get back,* we think. *I need to check in. I need to answer that email!*

We need a way to silence the inner murmur. "Come to me," Jesus says, "and I will give you rest."

The fourth commandment tells us to "Remember the Sabbath day by keeping it holy" (Exodus 20:8 NIV). It is a commandment to rest. But it comes with commentary: "For in six days the LORD made heaven and earth, the sea, and all that is in them, and rested on the seventh day. Therefore the LORD blessed the Sabbath day and made it holy" (v. 11). Do you see what's happening? Rest as I rested, says the Lord.

The fourth commandment points us back to the creation story, the story of the work and rest of God himself. Have you ever thought of it that way? The creation story shows us how God works and how God rests. It is mostly poetry—a song really. Genesis 1–2 is the song of God's wondrous activity.

Have you ever watched someone try to do too much? They never stop, never rest, and you say something like, "You're trying to be like God!" In one sense, this is true: they aren't living within their human limitations. But it isn't God they are trying to be like. God himself teaches us to model our work and rest after him. Eugene Peterson explains that if we are made in God's image, we should watch the creation week closely to see how God works.[8]

God doesn't pile all his work into one day, Peterson points out. Instead, he takes it one day at a time. He wants to enjoy it. First, he makes the sun and moon—night and day. That's a good first day. He stands back, like an artist from his work, squints, and says, "It's good." On the second day, he separates the water from the land. Again he takes note of the goodness of what he's done. On the third day he created plant life. On the fourth day, he made the stars and used the light to create seasons. On the fifth day, he made birds and swimming creatures, and on the sixth day, animals and his crowning achievement, humans. It was all good, he says. Very good.

God wasn't in a hurry, and he never procrastinated. Have you ever noticed that Jesus acted the same way? He healed lines of people, but then at some point in the day, he stopped, rested, prayed, and ate. He left many needs unattended. He was never in a hurry, and he never procrastinated. When we are in a hurry and never rest, we're not acting like God.

Watch me, God says. He worked six days and rested.

Why did God rest? Was he tired? No. God's rest is an image of divine satisfaction. He was enjoying what he had accomplished. "I don't have to do anything right now. It is finished. It's good." He had made little notations through the week of what was good, what went well—every blessing, every success, everything that was beautiful. God's rest was an act of fullness, joy, and delight. If God rested even though he wasn't tired and asks his image bearers to rest as he rested, do you think maybe there's a deeper reason for rest than just exhaustion?

Sabbath rest was so important for God that he set it apart. He memorialized it. He said, we need more of this! Genesis says,

"God blessed the seventh day and made it holy, because on it God rested from all his work that he had done in creation" (Genesis 2:3). God loves the Sabbath.

Abraham Heschel points out that the first holy object in the history of the world was not a place or something humans accomplished, but a day.[9] The first holy thing was not something we did but something to receive and participate in. That is counterintuitive to our modern thinking.

There's a pattern in Genesis 1. God created humans on the sixth day and gave them a job to do: rule over and subdue the earth. But the next day, they didn't get up and go to work because it was the seventh day, the day of rest. Only after that did the humans get to work. The first human act was not to work in order to rest but to rest, and *from that rest* they began their work. Isn't that surprising? "The Sabbath is the inspirer," Heschel says, "the other days the inspired."[10]

God was productive, creative, and worked hard, and he tells humans—who are made in his image—to do the same. The commandment to rest is God saying, "Work is not so important that you can't put it down. Only I am that important."

I want to connect the dots between the practice of Sabbath and the practice of prayer. The practice of Sabbath teaches us that nothing in this life is too important that it cannot be set aside in order to receive what God has for us rather than what we can make or do for ourselves. Our daily rhythms of prayer are small sabbaths—ways of saying to our soul, "Nothing is so important that it can't be regularly set aside to receive what God has for me today in his Word and in prayer."

OBSTACLES TO SABBATH

The first obstacle to Sabbath comes from an imbalanced relationship to work. If work is what ultimately provides meaning in our lives, we will not rest, even on our days off. We may be relaxing, we may be having fun, but what's humming under the hood of our hearts is the desire to get back, to get connected, to check in.

If we want to know whether our work has become the god of our lives, we can ask ourselves: *Have our days of rest become obstacles instead of joys?* If work is the very substance of our lives, what *defines* us, one or two things will inevitably happen. Either our work will crush us, or we will crush any and every relationship that gets in the way of our work. From my experience as a pastor, both are likely to occur.

Another obstacle to Sabbath is the pride of busyness. We love to tell others how busy we are, how much we work, how much we still have to get done, how overwhelmed we are by all our tasks. "How are you doing?" we are asked. "Busy!" we say. "Tired!" Why? Because if we were not so tired, busy, swamped, and exhausted, it would mean we are not that important or needed.

So we boast. We boast in how many emails we received, how many late nights we've had this week, how many trips are ahead. If I have enough time on my hands to take a day every week when I don't accomplish anything, I may not be as important or as needed as I think. The Sabbath humbles us. Heschel says that we must "learn to understand that the world has already been created and will survive without the help of man."[11] The Sabbath is our confession that the world is held together by Christ's hands, not ours.

A third obstacle is that many of us have *learned* to not rest. When our family first moved to New York City, I worked two jobs: I was a pastor and an editor. Days off were hard to come by and often hard to justify. That season lasted a few years. When I wasn't working, I felt guilty. Surely there was someone I needed to check in with, an email that needed responding to, a person who needed my help. My work habits were teaching my inner life that I shouldn't be taking time away. I always thought I was disappointing others, letting others down, and keeping people waiting.

Our work habits unconsciously teach us things we consciously know to be false, yet what we learn on the unconscious level drives our behavior and our emotional life more than what we know intellectually. Even after I went back to working just one job, that nagging guilt remained for a long time. I would be playing with my kids and have a sharp sense that I needed to check in. I would reach for my phone (or search for it). What was going on? The muscle memory of my heart still acted as if the pressures of two jobs were bearing down on me. Somewhere down deep, I had learned that work had to always be appeased. It had control over my inner life.

You don't have to work seventy or eighty hours a week for that to be true of you. You just need to ensure that you're always connected, always available, and never really resting—and the "eternal inner murmur of self-reproach" will shape your emotional and spiritual well-being.

Of course, our fears and insecurities come out in times of rest and stillness, so it's no surprise that many never want to stop. The ghosts and goblins come out when we are not busy proving ourselves. We are at the mercy of what we fear others might say or think of us—or what we might think of ourselves. We have to persevere very purposefully through some Sabbath days until our souls learn, little by little, to find their rest in God.

The goal of Sabbath is to give us a Sabbath of the heart so our souls can increasingly say,

I have calmed and quieted myself,
   I am like a weaned child with its mother;
   like a weaned child I am content. (Psalm 131:2 NIV)

This takes time, but it comes.

THE PRACTICE OF SABBATH

To be a healing and restorative practice, the Sabbath must be a weekly rhythm. We must figure out how to make time for a day once a week when we're not working but instead are putting joy and blessedness in the forefront. We trust that God has the universe under control, and we put everything down for a day. We seek out eating and drinking, we seek out our spouse, our children, our friendships. We seek to play and rest. The Lord says, "Remember the Sabbath day by keeping it holy" (Exodus 20:8 NIV). "Holy simply means set aside," says Dan Allender, "not lost in the sea of everything else."[12] The Sabbath is a day that looks different; it doesn't go along with the drive and drift of everyday life. It is holy: it is different, set aside.

One of the reasons the Sabbath is set aside is that the Lord blessed it (Genesis 2:3). It ought to be a rich day, intentionally full. It's a day that restores, renews, and heals. Think about this: What if the happiest and most powerful person in the universe came to us and said, "I want to give you a gift. It's something that I enjoy. It's something I cherish, and I want you to have it"? Can you imagine the anticipation we'd feel? This is exactly what the Sabbath is.

Then God says, "It's a day of rest, a Sabbath." And we say, "Oh. I don't have time for that, actually. It's not useful. I can't get things done by using the Sabbath." And we miss out.

God is giving us the biblical and theological justification to have the best day of the year every week, and we shrug. It turns out that if Sabbath rest is not already part of our lives, then it seems like an intruder.

Intentional preparation is helpful. Dan Allender compares preparing for the Sabbath to anticipating an honored guest: "Welcoming a guest moves from the heart to the hands. We must polish the brass, wash the linens, and clean the floors before our houseguest arrives. How would you prepare your home if an honored guest was about to arrive? You would make all the necessary preparations with the joy of anticipation. No mundane activities would take your attention away from your guest's arrival."[13]

So we prepare for the Sabbath as we would a cherished guest. We make arrangements. We get enough food, we get enough to drink, we prepare a room, we get things ready— not for drudgery but for joy! We make room in our week for the Sabbath. We plan ahead, we shift responsibilities, we make preparations. The best way to get a running start into Sabbath rhythms is to do it with others. Have Sabbath feasts. Be intentional in how you prepare for that day. Say to one another, "Today is for the purpose of joy and delight. We will set aside all that blinks, buzzes, or otherwise alerts us to things outside of joyful rest."

The Bible teaches us what kind of posture we ought to have during this day. In Exodus 20, when the Lord commands the people of Israel to remember the Sabbath day, he's reminding them of the days in the Garden of Eden—the original Sabbath, when God walked with Adam and Eve in the cool of the day. In Hebrews 4 the author tells us of a coming rest, a new world. "There *remains*, then, a Sabbath-rest for the people of God; for anyone who enters God's rest also rests from their works, just as God did from his. Let us, therefore, make every effort to enter that rest" (Hebrews 4:9-11 NIV). He's telling us to anticipate a day when we will be in full rest in the new heavens and new earth. That means that our Sabbath days now both *remember the Garden* and *rehearse the new creation*.[14]

REMEMBERING THE GARDEN

When God commands us to remember the Sabbath, he's inviting us to remember those original days in the Garden, the time of innocence and delight. In the Garden there was no grief, no sin, no worries, no anxieties, no division—only life and love. The Sabbath is a time to remember when humans didn't have to prove themselves worthy. Every day was a gift to receive. On the Sabbath we put down our inner need to overextend our competencies and prove ourselves. We rest with God and others.

I've picked up a practice that's helped me in Sabbath keeping. In the creation narrative God seems to be taking notes throughout the week about what's good, what to celebrate, and what worked. He created the sun—*it is good*; he made the stars and the moon—

they are good, he separated the earth from the sea, he made the animals, the birds, humankind—*they are all good*. It's as if he had a work journal so that by the end of the week he could step back, look over his notes, and say with a deep breath, "It's all *very* good."

So I began to do this myself. Each morning in my prayers, I would take a few minutes to write down what was good from my labors the previous day. What worked? What was worth celebrating? What was fruitful? What are the reasons to give thanks? Where was the Lord present? How was my work participating in what God was doing? At the end of the week our family brings in the Sabbath rest with a meal—a good dinner, something we all love, with special drinks around the table. Sometimes we share it with a few good friends. At dinner we each share what we're thankful for this week. We share what was worth celebrating and where we saw God's grace among us— and I have my list ready.

This is important because sometimes I can end the week feeling crushed by criticism, used by some, ignored by others, unworthy of love, and unfruitful in my work. I also have a tendency to grumble and to feel as if nothing good has come to me. But I have my list. And each Sabbath evening I sit down with my family with these notes of where "it was good"—where I have seen God at work, where my labors were fruitful, where the joy of the Lord was my strength. It helps me put down my work and rest.

REHEARSING THE NEW CREATION

To keep the Sabbath day holy is to rehearse the truth that someday God will make things right again. Justice will be restored, relationships will be reconciled, and our bodies will be healed. What we will be like, John the apostle tells us, we don't know, but what we do know is that "when he appears we shall be like him" (1 John 3:2). The world will be new, and we will be like Christ.

The Sabbath is a day to rehearse this truth. That means we treat those in our community as if they are who they will be in Christ, beautified in glory. We set aside tensions for the day. We assume the best of one another and give each other the benefit of the doubt. It doesn't mean that tensions and pain simply go away. It could be that we need to pick up those tensions the next day and work toward reconciliation. But letting what's eternally true in Christ (peace, reconciliation, and joy) inform for a day what is momentarily and experientially untrue now has a way of healing and restoring. Something of the kingdom breaks in and heals us.

It's a mystery, but it's God's way of doing things. Abraham Heschel tells a parable:

> A prince was once sent into captivity and compelled to live anonymously among rude and illiterate people. Years passed by, and he languished with longing for his royal father, for his native land. One day a secret communication reached him in which his father promised to bring him back to the palace, urging him not to unlearn his princely manner. Great was the joy of the prince, and he was eager to celebrate the day. But no one is able to celebrate alone. So he invited the people to the local tavern and ordered ample food and drinks for all of them. It was a sumptuous feast, and they were all full of rejoicing; the people because of the drinks and the prince in anticipation of his return to the palace.[15]

Do you see? The prince was rehearsing his princely manner and the joy of the palace so that he would not forget who he was called to be. That's the Sabbath. We rehearse what is coming—what is already true in Christ. We rehearse our princely manner so that we won't forget—because oh, how we forget.

The Sabbath is a remembrance of the Garden and a rehearsal of the new creation—of where we feasted with God in cool of the day and of where we will feast with him again in the new world. The Sabbath is a day for joy and delight. A day to buy too much food and share it. A day to eat, drink, and be merry because we're going to live forever!

The practice of a weekly Sabbath rest gives us a Sabbath heart. When Christ said, "It is finished" on the cross, God said, "It is good" over him. And remember what was said in chapter three, that everything that is true of Christ is true of us. When we are in Christ, what the Father says over the Son—"It is good"—is said over us too. We can work out of that rest.

When Christ said, "It is finished" on the cross, it was a death blow to finding our worth and fullness through our work. It means we can wake in the morning and not look immediately to work for worth, but instead come to Jesus in his Word and prayer and receive all the fullness as a gift. When Jesus said, "It is finished," it meant that in the eyes of the One whose opinion truly matters, you and I are pleasing and satisfying. When the Father sees me, when he sees you, he says, "It is good." Do you believe that? Practicing the Sabbath is the rhythm of strangling that "inner murmur" with worship and joy.

CHAPTER TWELVE

CORPORATE WORSHIP

OUR BRAINS HAVE TWO BASIC STATES: sympathetic ("engaged" mode) and parasympathetic ("relaxation" mode). These two states are responsible for how our bodies process different experiences and automate things like digestion, blood pressure, and sweat.

Prayer ordinarily leads to a parasympathetic response, reducing our blood pressure and stress and leading to a relaxed state.[1] However, in deep, attentive, and focused prayer, or in corporate worship, both systems are active at once. "Generally speaking," says neuroscientist Andrew Newberg, "it is rare that an experience both arouses and calms, which is one of the reasons why we think spiritual experience stimulates the brain in a unique way."[2]

"Worship can be loud and exciting while also creating a sense of inner peace," the writer Rob Moll observes. "Or it may be intellectually stimulating while being relaxing, not taxing. The more that the two systems are simultaneously engaged, the more profound the experience. And when this spiritual circuit is fully engaged, we can experience a feeling of union with God and often with other people as well."[3] Both attentive prayer and corporate worship activate every part of our brains. The frontal lobe "is rationally thinking about the experience, understanding it in terms of theology and application"; the limbic system "helps to provide an emotional flavor to the experience. At the same time, the *amygdala*, which is often the center of our experiences of fear and anger, might be soothed or calmed"; and the anterior cingulate "would help to translate these thoughts and emotions into compassion and empathy toward other people."[4] "Some have argued," says Moll, "that spirituality is a hallucination or caused by epilepsy. But unlike those dysfunctions, spirituality seems to enhance the brain's capacity in a number of ways, it has healthful effects on the rest of the body, and it is personally meaningful."[5]

This is your brain on prayer and worship. And while we are certainly more than brains and neurons, we are embodied creatures. The research of Andrew Newberg and Rob Moll shows us that our bodies and brains are witnesses that we are made for transcendent realities and are physically affected by the spiritual habit of prayer. Seeing what happens to our physical bodies and brains in attentive prayer and corporate worship demonstrates that this is how God has designed us to experience the world. "The body," as writer and pastor Peter Scazzero says, "is a major, not a minor prophet."[6] "Researchers have found that spiritual activity, such as prayer, enhances our brain's ability to recognize the suffering of others and to respond in action. The areas of the brain involved in spirituality tend to strengthen those involved in compassion."[7]

Long before we could study the brain, the Bible taught that the normal way to experience intimacy with God and transformation is through a life of prayer.

We want to be holy as God is holy; we want to be humble as Christ is humble; we want to care for the lowly as God cares for the lowly. But our actual character does not match our beliefs about what our character should be. The two need to be reconciled. The ordinary way we bridge these two realities is through prayer. But Scripture also aims us toward habits that enhance the power of prayer in our lives, like Sabbath resting, fasting, and feasting. These are not mere suggestions to supplement prayer but the actual vehicle of the power and life that sustain our spiritual life with God that he has designed us to engage in. They use deep mechanisms of change and put us in the way of transformation.

Corporate worship—the weekly gathering together with other Christians—is one of those habits. Corporate worship uses deeper mechanisms of change because it is not a habit that aims directly at self-improvement but at enjoyment. Worship is a command to enjoy an object. We are stirred toward desiring and loving God. But when we aim our love and desires toward God, we are changed. Corporate worship results in deep transformation because it aims at deep desires and draws us into participation with deep realities. Worship, and particularly corporate worship, is a spiritual rhythm of great importance.

The individualistic streak in American Christianity balks at the importance of corporate worship. "As long as my relationship with Jesus is good, I'm good," we say. But the New Testament doesn't allow for that. The more we are alienated from other Christians, the more we will be alienated from Christ himself. It's a mystery, but that's how God has put it all together. We simply cannot depend on a personal prayer life for a healthy spiritual life—or even an adequate one. Without other Christians and the experience of worshiping with them on a regular basis, our personal prayer lives will suffer. We need corporate worship. We need to gather regularly with other Christians to sing, pray, read, and hear God's Word, to receive the Lord's Supper, and to be sent back into the world full of peace and good news.

The most common psalm that the early Christian church used as a call to worship—the part of the service that calls and focuses the worshipers—was Psalm 95.

> Oh come, let us sing to the LORD;
>> let us make a joyful noise to the rock of our salvation!
> Let us come into his presence with thanksgiving;
>> let us make a joyful noise to him with songs of praise!
> For the LORD is a great God,
>> and a great King above all gods. (Psalm 95:1-3)

From the very beginning, this psalm commands us to sing—and to sing together. "Let *us* sing." Christians have always been a singing people. It's who we are. In fact, one of the most common commands in Scripture is to sing. Have you ever noticed that? It's surprising that it's not more common to read commands to offer sacrifices, to give our money or time, or to do some other act of service. That's what we'd expect because that's how our relationships often function. They are transactional. You scratch my back, I'll scratch yours. But God's relationship with us has never been transactional.

In the Bible everything seems to sing. Angels sing (Job 38:7; Psalm 148:2; 103:20; Revelation 5:8-11), rocks cry out (Luke 19:40), the stars declare God's glory (Psalm 19:1), and even the mountains sing (Psalm 98:8; Isaiah 55:12). If God is who he says he is, then singing is the most rational thing. To sing is to join ourselves to ultimate reality—to join ourselves with everything that isn't asleep. Singing is a declaration that we are awake to reality, awake to God and to our life with him. To not sing is to be out of sync with reality, to miss something fundamental not just about ourselves but about all of creation. To live without singing of our delight in God is like driving a car in second gear; you can drive it that way, but you'll never open yourself up to the pleasure of driving down the open road with the engine at full capacity.

"Let us come into his presence with thanksgiving" (Psalm 95:2). This talk about presence can be intimidating to us. It causes some of us to hesitate rather than to come with thanksgiving. Maybe we've been struggling with a particular sin this week. Being around God's people and God's presence feels invasive, not inviting. It reminds us of how much we've failed. We're not holy enough. Or maybe we've had a pretty good week, and we feel confident. We look at other Christians and we feel up to snuff.

Neither of these postures has the singing heart the psalmist calls for. They both assume that our invitation into worship is based on what we deserve. But Christian worship is based on grace. The psalmist never says "Come, let us make a sacrifice so that we may come into his presence to sing." He says, "Come into his presence with thanksgiving." The sacrifice of Christ already makes us clean.

Which means we come with our *emotions*: "sing," "make a joyful noise," "with thanksgiving." Then the psalmist says, "bow down . . . kneel before the LORD, our Maker," come with your *will*. "Today," he says, "if you hear his voice," listen, come with your *mind*. The invitation to worship is an invitation to our whole selves.

We come with our whole selves and give our attention to him. "In his hand," the psalmist says in Psalm 95:4, "are the depths of the earth; the heights of the mountains are his also." The Old Testament scholar Arthur Weiser says this verse is a *counterworship*. In the time of the psalmist, Weiser says, "there were popular beliefs that other powers resided in the underworld (the depths) and the lesser gods infiltrated the skies (the mountains). This Psalm deliberately destroys this belief. God is the ruler of all."[8] In other words, there were certain gods you had to appease in order to get what you wanted in life—the harvest gods for good crops, the rain gods to defend against drought, and regional gods of other parts of the country if you were traveling. You had to delegate your devotion in order to get what you wanted out of life—a little here, a little there.

That may sound archaic to us. We are modern people who don't believe in that sort of spirituality. But it may not be as far off the mark as we think. There may not be a harvest god or a rain god, but for many of us there are career gods, money gods, beauty gods, and relationship gods, and we delegate our devotion in order to get what we want from each. We may believe in the Christian God, but our lives are not fully given to him. We give a little of our life here, a little of our devotion there. God has part of our devotion but not all of it. And let's be honest, since we're doing the delegating, we're in control.

True worship combats this impulse. It comes into God's presence with singing and thanksgiving, with our whole lives, with our undelegated devotion. This is the God who made heaven and earth, and he's calling for our whole attention. Not only is he worthy of it, but we won't be happy unless we give it.

Much of this book is concerned with the rhythms and habits we practice alone. Corporate worship, of course, is done with others. "Let *us* sing," says the psalmist. The Bible is describing a practice that cannot be done alone. That may sound obvious, but it's striking how much of the Christian life we think we can do alone when it's clearly impossible. Fulfilling even the basic commands of loving others, bearing one another's burdens, and forgiving others cannot be accomplished alone. These commands assume that others will be in our lives as objects of our love—people to whom we're close enough to experience their sin and they our forgiveness. Much of the Christian life cannot be done in isolation. Corporate worship is the culmination of everything that's happening together in the believing community.

Augustine used the Latin phrase *totus Christus*, "the whole Christ," to describe this spiritual dynamic. "The whole Christ" means that as Christians, we need all of Christ, both the head (Christ himself) and the body (the church).[9] Corporate worship is the place where the *totus Christus* is most fully expressed. In worship, Christ is present with his body corporately and with each individual member as the individual members experience Christ by way of his corporate body. There is more going on in corporate worship than we often think, and there are deeper realities we ought to be alert to when we are *with Christ* and *with his body* in worship.

WITH CHRIST

The central reality of corporate worship is the *real presence of Christ*—the doctrine that in worship Christ is really present with us by the power of the Holy Spirit. "When you are assembled in the name of the Lord Jesus and my spirit is present, with the power of our Lord Jesus" (1 Corinthians 5:4). When we gather together, Christ gathers with us in power. This power is not subtle; it is his creative, transforming power. The same power that knocked Saul of Tarsus to the ground and struck him blind comes to church with us on Sunday. That means that, as the theologian John Jefferson Davis puts it, "in every true worship assembly the Damascus Road reality can be available to impact and transform the believing church by faith."[10] Paul says in 1 Corinthians 14:25 that "God is really among you."

We have been raised with Christ and seated with him in the heavenly places (Ephesians 2:6-7), and what is true of Christ in his death, resurrection, and glory is true of us (Colossians 3:1-4). The risen and glorified Christ is present with us in corporate worship, where we experience the powers of the age to come today (Hebrews 6:5)! The promised glorious future is not just a hope we talk and pray about but something we taste and see by way of the real presence of Christ when we gather to worship. The potential for delight and transformation is infinite.

So corporate worship isn't an escape from the monotony or hurriedness of real life. Because of the real presence of Christ by the Spirit in the midst of his people, worship is "more intensely real than ordinary life."[11] The "eternal weight of glory" (2 Corinthians 4:17) has dwelt among us, with all the density of heaven itself. When we gather to worship together, our first act is to acknowledge this reality.

WITH HIS BODY

Jesus tells us that we are connected to him like a branch to a vine. The vine (Christ) is connected to the branches (us), and the life and power that runs through the vine go into the branches. Insofar as the branch abides in the vine, the branch flourishes.

Paul says that we have been "called in one body" (Colossians 3:15). The language of body is a more complex image of how we are connected to Christ than the vine and branches. When we become Christians we are not only vitally connected to Christ (like a branch to a vine), we become a part of a body (with other Christians) that is connected to the head (with Christ). The same vitality that runs through the head runs through the body, similar to the vine-branch dynamic. The only difference is that as members of a body, we need the rest of the body in order to experience the vitality of the head.

One profound way to experience the body of Christ is through corporate prayer. This point in the service can be awkward for some simply because the prayers can be concerned with things we're not concerned with at the moment. Or maybe we're not feeling the emotion of a particular prayer. Maybe we've come to church after a week of success and victory at work, and we're feeling great. But the prayer is a lament—grief over the loss and trouble of this world. Our immediate response may be,

I don't need this! I've had a great week. But it's likely that more than a few of the people around us are experiencing trouble, maybe even great suffering. Corporate prayer is an opportunity to enter into the trials and griefs of others, even if it's just for a moment. Or it could be that we do feel grief and loss, but the prayers are all full of joy and confidence. Prayer is an opportunity to rejoice with others, even when we don't feel the same emotions. Corporate prayer is a way to practice the basic empathy of the Christian life: "Rejoice with those who rejoice, weep with those who weep" (Romans 12:15).

In the human body there are systems at work: the circulatory system circulates the blood, the respiratory system carries oxygen, the digestive system breaks down food so the body can absorb nutrients, and the nervous system sends its signals to the rest of the body so we can interact with the physical world around us. If any part of the body is hindered from the benefit of any of these systems, it withers and dies. We need the other parts of the body in order to flourish and be healthy. So it is in the body of Christ, his church. We wither when we try to live apart from other Christians. Something of the power and transforming life of Christ is lost when we do not gather with other believers.

We don't know how this works, but there are certain joys and wonders that we cannot have unless we gather with other brothers and sisters in Christ.

Paul says we are "called in one body" (Colossians 3:15). We gather together because we are called to it. The language of calling carries a sense of vocation. I live in a city where hundreds of thousands of people come to follow a calling. They come to work on

Broadway, Wall Street, the fashion industry, film, or music. To be called is to have a sense of inner obligation toward something, which leaves us restless until we accomplish it, until we've *made it*.

The New Testament calls us toward something deeper than that. We have been called to a body. If you've ever wondered what God wants for your life, here is at least a partial answer: to be deeply connected and involved in the body of Christ. You won't be satisfied until you are. That's how callings work. If we aren't working toward our calling, we feel out of place, always a bit off. And the reason I say *deeper* calling is because it's deeper than a feeling or an intuition about a direction in our life. This isn't a feeling, because we often do not *feel* like being sacrificially involved and deeply connected in the lives of others. But since it's deeper than a feeling, it provides deeper satisfaction than a feeling can.

Our spiritual lives are not hindered but are enhanced by other Christians. In fact, individual Christians suffer when corporate worship is an irregular rhythm—and, in fact, the body suffers when you do not gather with them. I wonder if you think about it that way. Do you ever consider that your absence is a hindrance to the health of the body? Whether you are a leader or a new believer, you have been called to the body, and that calling is not only for your own good but also for the good of others. The corporate gathering is the consummation of what has been happening in the *totus Christus* during the rest of the week. The power, life, and vitality of Christ come to us personally through the presence of Christ and corporately through the body. We need both.

One of the aims of corporate worship is *inner truthfulness*. "Do not harden your hearts," says the psalmist (Psalm 95:8). Then he reminds his readers of a time when the people's hearts were hardened: "as at Meribah, as on the day at Massah in the wilderness, when you fathers put me to the test and put me to the proof, though they had seen my work" (vv. 8-9). The psalmist is reminding them of a time in the history of Israel, after they were freed from slavery, when they were wandering through the wilderness. God had worked powerful wonders to deliver the Israelites from slavery, but they had a short memory. They began to grumble. They wondered aloud, "Is the Lord among us or not?"

The names of the place, Meribah and Massah, were given by God, and they mean "Grumbling" and "Testing." Grumbling is the opposite of worship. It's different from the places of lament and complaint in Psalms and other parts of the Bible where we bring our emotions, frustrations, and even anger to God. That isn't what's happening at Meribah. The people hardened their hearts and grumbled among themselves. God wasn't living up to their expectations, and they'd had enough. Despite what God had done for them—the miracles of their deliverance from Egypt—they still wondered whether he would be there for them. God was on constant probation.

Psalm 95 recalls this story because, though we may not be in a physical wilderness, our circumstances will sometimes be like the Israelites', and we need to be aware. When the psalmist calls us to worship, it's not superficial cheerfulness. The context for this kind of worship is not merely the abundance of God's blessing. This kind of worship is for the wilderness of life. In the heat of the wilderness the truthfulness of our hearts comes out. The pressures of the wilderness brought out grumbling and testing in the Israelites, and the question that Psalm 95 wants us to consider is, When you're experiencing the pressures and pains of the wilderness, what comes out?

The circumstances of the Israelites' lives shaped how they related to God rather than their relationship with God shaping the way they encountered the circumstances of their life. Worship teaches us how to do the latter. The Israelites had certain expectations of God, a picture of what life ought to be like with him. And since he did not fit into their imaginations, they did not trust him. They were testing him—but they were testing him according to their own standards, not his.

Corporate worship sings about the true character of God: his mercy and love, his grace and patience. Worship is meditating on the greatness of God and treasuring his excellences. It replaces our small and deficient expectations of God, even if they were subconscious, and replaces them with something more substantial and stable. It teaches our hearts to say, "If he's been good thus far, then I'm sure he will be with me in this trouble too, and what he has for me is greater than what I can provide for myself." This way, when the wilderness pressures come—and they will—what comes out of us will be a joy that runs deeper and lasts longer than the trouble.

The presence of Christ is the fundamental reality of all worship. The more intentionally and consciously we press into it, the greater our existential grasp of it will be, so whether in pain or comfort, trouble or joy, we will know that Christ is with us. And if Christ is with us, what can human beings do to us? "They will have no fear of bad news; their hearts are steadfast, trusting in the LORD" (Psalm 112:7 NIV).

Amen. Let it be so.

CONCLUSION

IT IS QUIET NOW that everyone has gone to bed. It's been a long day, full of meetings, school events, emails, subway rides, and errands. Some days when I come home, I need to take a deep breath right before I open the door and enter a new kind of fullness: dinner preparations, helping with homework, playing, dishes, breaking up little arguments, and asking for forgiveness for my impatience. But now, finally, it's quiet. I'm tired. I need to sleep well tonight—but not yet.

I have the book of Psalms by my bed. I open it. Tonight's reading is Psalm 90. "Satisfy us . . . with your steadfast love" (v. 14). Yes, I need that. Earlier in the passage, the psalmist complained a bit that life has seemed meaningless. "For all our days pass away under your wrath; we bring our years to an end like a sigh" (Psalm 90:9). Life is short, he says, and it's all "toil and trouble" (v. 10).

Some days can feel like that, can't they? Days end with a *sigh*. "Well, I'm glad that's over." Except tomorrow doesn't look much different. Toil and trouble are not life-giving phenomena. Toil is pointless work, and trouble is, well, trouble. If I'm being honest, I can admit this to the Lord. "What's the point?" I say. Satisfy us with your steadfast love.

Maybe you aren't feeling the emotion of this psalm when you open to it, but others in your life likely are. It's a good time to pray for them. Lift them up; pray for their comfort, healing, and joy. Sometimes people just need a breakthrough in life, and prayer is an ordinary means by which God does just that.

Often the Psalms show us what emotions we *ought* to be feeling when we are not. Dietrich Bonhoeffer writes, "If we were dependent entirely on ourselves, we would probably pray only the fourth petition of the Lord's Prayer [Give us our daily bread]. But God wants it otherwise. The richness of the Word of God ought to determine our prayer, not the poverty of our heart."[1] The apostle John tells us, "Whenever our heart condemns us, God is greater than our heart, and he knows everything" (1 John 3:20). If we're ending our day with feelings and emotions of guilt, God has something better for us to go to bed with. Don't go to bed with whatever impoverished feelings, emotions, or mixed voices from the day that linger in our hearts. "It does not depend, therefore, on whether the Psalms express adequately that which we feel at a given moment in our heart," Bonhoeffer goes on. "If we are to pray aright, perhaps it is quite necessary that we pray contrary to our own heart."[2]

The psalmist keeps going, "Return, O Lord! How long?" (Psalm 90:13). He begins to turn toward his longings: "Satisfy us in the morning with your steadfast love" (v. 14). I'm going to bed tonight full of trouble and toil. Meet me in the morning, Lord. When I awake, I want to rejoice and be glad with you. The psalmist goes on to pray, "Establish the work of our hands upon us" (v. 17). Tomorrow is a new day with new mercies, so the psalmist asks that God would fill his work with substance and meaning.

These are good, ordinary prayers that God answers. I pray the Psalms at the end of the day because I want to go to bed with God's perspective on my day that's ending and with the hope that God has for tomorrow.

In John Updike's novel *Rabbit Redux*, the second book in his Rabbit trilogy, a young, runaway hippy named Jill is talking to Harry "Rabbit" Angstrom, now in middle age. She's explaining how his "American pragmatism" had turned to cynicism:

> We all agree, I think, that your problem is that you've never been given a chance to formulate your views. Because of the competitive American context, you've had to convert everything into action too rapidly. Your life has no reflective content; it's all instinct, and when your instincts let you down, you have nothing to trust. That's what makes you cynical. Cynicism, I've seen it said somewhere, is tired pragmatism. Pragmatism suited a certain moment here, the frontier moment; it did the work, very wastefully and ruthlessly, but it did it.[3]

"Your life has no reflective content; it's all instinct." That sentence from 1971 could just as easily be said of many of us today. We've had to "convert everything into action too rapidly," and now we feel tossed by every changing circumstance in our lives. We've formed reactionary hearts rather than hearts at rest, driven by something deeper and more eternal than the moment by moment changes in our lives.

It's hard to love others deeply with reactionary hearts. It's difficult to experience gratitude when we live merely off instinct and impulse. The practice of prayer breaks the cycle of instinct and impulse and teaches us to pay attention to how God has been lovingly present with us all along and how our friends and family need our love and presence.

It's no overstatement to say that the most transformative thing you can do is to begin to spend unhurried time with God on a regular basis for the rest of your life. Maybe you began this book doubtful that a vibrant life of prayer is for you. Maybe you've had many starts and stops. What I've been trying to show in this book is that consistent prayer is possible. My hope is that these reflections have stirred not only a desire to continue in prayer but shared wisdom for the path ahead and strategies for perseverance.

ACKNOWLEDGMENTS

I'M GRATEFUL FOR the people and leaders at Apostles Church in New York City. Their regular encouragement, prayers, and the provided sabbatical made this book a reality. I came back from my sabbatical with a finished manuscript and a lot of gratitude. I owe quite a bit of debt to John Beeson, who regularly checked in and read my manuscript with detailed feedback. I'm grateful for Philip Revell, Jamie Leahy, Ryan Taylor, Adam Gahagan, Freeman Field, Mike Cosper, Keren Baltzer, Don Gates, Ethan McCarthy, and Christina Gilliland, who all helped me along the way, from the beginning idea to the final product. There were others, too many to mention here, who gave encouragement as this project progressed.

A owe a deeper gratitude to two people who shaped this book more than others. First, my wife, Jena. She read through my material and gave critical feedback that was crucial to how everything ended up. She didn't allow me to get away with anything that didn't seem to come from my true voice. She made this book harder to write but better in the end. So much of this material came from our lives and ministry together.

Finally, I need to acknowledge my debt to Eugene Peterson. Peterson passed on to his inheritance during the writing of this book. It would be hard to summarize how he has impacted my vocation as a minister and the material of this book. His life and work was a witness to the long obedience. I pray this book merely follows along in the way that he was going. I dedicate it to his memory.

NOTES

INTRODUCTION

[1]Hans Urs von Balthasar, *Prayer* (San Francisco: Ignatius Press, 1986), 23.

[2]Oscar Wilde, *The Picture of Dorian Gray* (New York: Modern Library, 1998), xii.

1 THE IMPOSSIBILITY OF PRAYER

[1]Annie Dillard, *Teaching a Stone to Talk: Expeditions and Encounters* (New York: Harper Perennial, 1988), 14.

[2]Thomas Nagel, *What Does It All Mean? A Very Short Introduction to Philosophy* (Oxford: Oxford University Press, 1987), 17.

[3]Alison Gopnik, "How an 18th-Century Philosopher Helped Solve My Midlife Crisis," *Atlantic*, October 2015, www.theatlantic.com/magazine/archive/2015/10/how-david -hume-helped-me-solve-my-midlife-crisis/403195.

[4]Ignatius of Antioch, quoted in Olivier Clément, *The Roots of Christian Mysticism: Texts from the Patristic Era with Commentary*, 2nd ed. (New York: New City Press, 2013), 36.

[5]Dillard, *Teaching a Stone to Talk*, 26.

[6]Hans Urs von Balthasar, *Prayer* (San Francisco: Ignatius Press, 1986), 165.

[7]Much of the remainder of this chapter also appears in John Starke, "Spiritual Pride and Reading the Gospels Well," *Gospel Coalition*, December 28, 2015, www.thegospelcoalition .org/article/spiritual-pride-and-reading-the-gospels-well.

[8]Henri J. M. Nouwen, *The Road to Daybreak: A Spiritual Journey* (New York: Image, 1990), 84.

[9]Nouwen, *Road to Daybreak*, 84.

2 THE PLACES OF PRAYER

[1]This section is helped along by John Jefferson Davis, *Worship and the Reality of God: An Evangelical Theology of Real Presence* (Downers Grove, IL: IVP Academic, 2010), 48-60.

[2]Davis, *Worship and the Reality of God*, 49.

[3]Jonathan D. Teubner, *Prayer After Augustine: A Study in the Development of the Latin Tradition* (Oxford: Oxford University Press, 2018), 37-49. Teubner's work was a great help in the development of this section.

[4]Teubner, *Prayer After Augustine*, 49.

3 THE INVITATION OF PRAYER

[1]Annie Dillard, *The Writing Life* (New York: HarperPerennial, 1995), 68-69.

[2]Eugene H. Peterson, *God's Message for Each Day: Wisdom from the Word of God* (Nashville: Thomas Nelson, 2006), 30.

[3]Louise Penny, *Still Life* (New York: St. Martin's Minotaur, 2006), 205.

[4]James Baldwin, *The Price of the Ticket: Collected Nonfiction, 1948-1985* (New York: St. Martin's/Marek, 1985), 375.

⁵Hans Urs von Balthasar, *Prayer* (San Francisco: Ignatius Press, 1986), 77.
⁶Balthasar, *Prayer*, 78.

4 OUTGROWING THE REACTIONARY HEART

¹Henri J. M. Nouwen, *Reaching Out: The Three Movements of the Spiritual Life* (New York: Image, 1975), 50.
²See David G. Benner, *Soulful Spirituality: Becoming Fully Alive and Deeply Human* (Grand Rapids: Brazos, 2011).
³Benner, *Soulful Spirituality*, 44.
⁴Benner, *Soulful Spirituality*, 45.
⁵Benner, *Soulful Spirituality*, 46.
⁶Derek Kidner, *Psalms 1–72*, Kidner Classic Commentaries (Downers Grove, IL: IVP Academic, 2014), 176.
⁷Athanasius, quoted in Eugene H. Peterson, *Working the Angles: The Shape of Pastoral Integrity* (Grand Rapids: Eerdmans, 2001), 55.
⁸Eugene H. Peterson, *Answering God: The Psalms as a Tool of Prayer* (New York: Harper-Collins, 1992), 7.

5 PAIN AND PRAYER

¹Henri J. M. Nouwen, *The Road to Daybreak: A Spiritual Journey* (New York: Image Books, 1990), 25–26.
²Approximately the first third of this chapter also appears in John Starke, "When Healing Takes Time," *Gospel Coalition*, September 23, 2015, www.thegospelcoalition.org/article/when-healing-takes-time.
³Nouwen, *Road to Daybreak*, 26.
⁴Nouwen. *Road to Daybreak*, 68.
⁵Hans Urs von Balthasar, *Prayer* (San Francisco: Ignatius Press, 1986), 25.
⁶Charles Taylor, *A Secular Age* (Harvard, MA: Belknap Press, 2018), 309.
⁷Jean-Paul Sartre, *No Exit and Three Other Plays* (New York: Vintage International, 1989).
⁸Dan B. Allender, *Leading with a Limp : Take Full Advantage of Your Most Powerful Weakness* (Colorado Springs, CO: Waterbrook Press, 2008), 69.
⁹Nouwen, *Road to Daybreak*, 146.
¹⁰Nouwen, *Road to Daybreak*, 174.

6 WAITING AND PRAYER

¹Kenneth Grahame, *The Wind in the Willows* (London: Egmont, 2016), 88–91. A few Christians have worried that Grahame was attempting to evoke paganism and the worship of the god Pan, who comforts lost animals. But like many other authors, from Tolkien to Lewis, Grahame is imaginatively employing myths to show us the truth.
²Henri Nouwen, quoted in Christopher Hall, *Worshiping with the Church Fathers* (Downers Grove, IL: IVP Academic, 2009), 91.
³Hall, *Worshiping with the Church Fathers*, 92.
⁴Hall, *Worshiping with the Church Fathers*, 96.
⁵Ronald Rolheiser, *Sacred Fire: A Vision for a Deeper Human and Christian Maturity* (New York: Doubleday, 2017), 74.

⁶See Rolheiser, *Sacred Fire*, 104-5.

⁷Rolheiser, *Sacred Fire*, 104.

⁸Olivier Clément, *The Roots of Christian Mysticism : Texts from the Patristic Era with Commentary* (New York: New City Press, 2014), 189-90.

⁹Clément, *The Roots of Christian Mysticism*, 189.

¹⁰See Rolheiser, *Sacred Fire*, 151-54.

¹¹Rolheiser, *Sacred Fire*, 152.

¹²Rolheiser, *Sacred Fire*, 152-53.

PART 2: THE PRACTICE OF PRAYER

¹Bertrand Russell, "What Desires Are Politically Important?" *NobelPrize.org*, December 11, 1950, www.nobelprize.org/prizes/literature/1950/russell/lecture.

7 COMMUNION

¹Ronald Rolheiser, *Sacred Fire: A Vision for a Deeper Human and Christian Maturity* (New York: Doubleday, 2017), 181.

²Augustine, quoted in Olivier Clément, *The Roots of Christian Mysticism: Texts from the Patristic Era with Commentary* (New York: New City Press, 2014), 181-82.

³Clément. *Roots of Christian Mysticism*, 561.

8 MEDITATION

¹Eugene Peterson, *Eat This Book : A Conversation in the Art of Spiritual Reading* (Grand Rapids: Eerdmans, 2006), 30.

²Bruce Springsteen, "Glory Days," *Born in the U.S.A.*, recorded 1982; released 1985, Columbia Records.

³See Richard F. Lovelace, *Dynamics of Spiritual Life: An Evangelical Theology of Renewal* (Downers Grove, IL: InterVarsity Press, 1979), 31.

⁴Hans Urs von Balthasar, *Prayer* (San Francisco: Ignatius Press, 1986), 18.

⁵Balthasar, *Prayer*, 17.

9 SOLITUDE

¹Sam Anderson, "New Sentences: From 'Nicotine,' by Nell Zink," *New York Times Magazine*, May 14, 2017, 13.

²Annie Dillard. *Pilgrim at Tinker Creek* (New York: Harper Perennial, 2013), 11.

³Bernard of Clairvaux, *On Consideration* (Oxford: Clarendon Press, 1908), 158.

⁴John Owen, *The Works of John Owen*, ed. William H. Goold (Edinburgh: Banner of Truth Trust, 2000), 6:83.

⁵C. S. Lewis, *Letters to Children* (New York: Simon & Schuster, 1996), 26-27.

⁶Benjamin Baird, Jonathan Smallwood, and Jonathan W. Schooler, "Back to the Future: Autobiographical Planning and the Functionality of Mind-Wandering," *Consciousness and Cognition* 20 (2011): 1604-11.

⁷Henri J. M. Nouwen, *Reaching Out: The Three Movements of the Spiritual Life* (New York: Image, 1975), 37-38.

⁸Sherry Turkle, *Reclaiming Conversation: The Power of Talk in a Digital Age* (New York: Penguin, 2015), 10, Kindle.

⁹Turkle, *Reclaiming Conversation*, 10.

¹⁰Nouwen, *Reaching Out*, 34.

¹¹Nir Eyal, *Hooked: How to Build Habit-Forming Products* (New York: Penguin, 2014), 14.

¹²Alexis C. Madrigal, "The Machine Zone: This Is Where You Go When You Just Can't Stop Looking at Pictures on Facebook," *Atlantic*, July 31, 2013, www.theatlantic.com /technology/archive/2013/07/the-machine-zone-this-is-where-you-go-when-you-just -cant-stop-looking-at-pictures-on-facebook/278185.

¹³Mark W. Becker, Reem Alzahabi, and Christopher J. Hopwood, "Media Multitasking Is Associated with Symptoms of Depression and Social Anxiety," *Cyberpsychology, Behavior, and Social Networking* 16, no. 2 (2012): 132-35.

¹⁴For more see Daphna Shohamy, Raphael Gerraty, Gloria Mark Dimitrios Tsivrikos, and Genevieve Bell, "The Case for Infomagical," *Note to Self*, January 24, 2016, www.wnyc.org /story/case-infomagical.

¹⁵Thomas Merton, *New Seeds of Contemplation* (New York: New Directions, 2007), 54.

10 FASTING AND FEASTING

¹Robert Farrar Capon, *The Supper of the Lamb: A Culinary Reflection* (New York: Modern Library, 2002), 112-15.

²Capon, *Supper of the Lamb*, 113.

³Capon, *Supper of the Lamb*, 114.

⁴Capon, *Supper of the Lamb*, 114.

⁵Capon, *Supper of the Lamb*, 115.

⁶Thomas Merton, *New Seeds of Contemplation* (New York: New Directions, 2007), 51, Kindle.

⁷Merton, *New Seeds of Contemplation*, 51.

⁸Capon, *Supper of the Lamb*, 40.

⁹Capon, *Supper of the Lamb*, 40.

11 SABBATH RESTING

¹Philo, *De Specialibus Legibus*, 11.60, quoted in Abraham Joshua Heschel, *The Sabbath*, FSG Classics (New York: Farrar, Straus and Giroux, 2005), loc. 1153-54, Kindle.

²Heschel, *Sabbath*, loc. 276-277.

³Judith Shulevitz, *The Sabbath World: Glimpses of a Different Order of Time* (New York: Random House, 2010), loc. 558-60, Kindle.

⁴Shulevitz, *Sabbath World*, loc. 560-66.

⁵Shulevitz, *Sabbath World*, loc. 579.

⁶Shulevitz, *Sabbath World*, loc. 618-19.

⁷Judith Shulevitz, "Bring Back the Sabbath." *New York Times Magazine*, March 2, 2003, www.nytimes.com/2003/03/02/magazine/bring-back-the-sabbath.html.

⁸Eugene Peterson, *Christ Plays in Ten Thousand Places: A Conversation in Spiritual Theology* (Grand Rapids: Eerdmans, 2008), 65-82.

⁹Heschel, *Sabbath*, loc. 236-37.

¹⁰Heschel, *Sabbath*, loc. 262.

¹¹Heschel, *Sabbath*, loc. 262.

[12]Dan B. Allender, *Sabbath* (Nashville: Thomas Nelson, 2009), 37.

[13]Allender, *Sabbath*, 60-61.

[14]Allender regularly touches on this theme: "The Sabbath is a feast that remembers our leisure in Eden and anticipates our play in the new heavens and earth with family, friends, and strangers for the sake of the glory of God" (*Sabbath*, loc. 144). Allender doesn't necessarily ground this theme in Exodus 20 or Hebrews 4, but it's certainly there, and it inspired the following reflection on what it actually looks like to remember the Garden and rehearse the new creation.

[15]Heschel, *Sabbath*, loc. 346.

12 CORPORATE WORSHIP

[1]Andrew Newberg, Eugene d'Aquili, and Vince Rause, *Why God Won't Go Away: Brain Science and the Biology of Belief* (New York: Ballantine Books, 2001), 86-90, cited in Rob Moll, *What Your Body Knows About God: How We Are Designed to Connect, Serve and Thrive* (Downers Grove, IL: InterVarsity Press, 2014), 203, Kindle.

[2]Andrew Newberg and Mark Robert Waldman, *How God Changes Your Brain* (New York: Ballantine, 2010), 26-27, quoted in Moll, *What Your Body Knows About God*, 23.

[3]Moll, *What Your Body Knows About God*, 23.

[4]Newberg and Waldman, *How God Changes Your Brain*, 124-26, cited in Moll, *What Your Body Knows About God*, 24.

[5]Moll, *What Your Body Knows About God*, 24.

[6]Peter Scazzero, *The Emotionally Healthy Leader: How Transforming Your Inner Life Will Deeply Transform Your Church, Team, and the World* (Grand Rapids: Zondervan, 2015), 321.

[7]Moll, *What Your Body Knows About God*, 31.

[8]Artur Weiser, *The Psalms: A Commentary* (Philadelphia: Westminster Press, 2010), 636.

[9]See Jonathan D. Teubner, *Prayer After Augustine: A Study in the Development of the Latin Tradition* (Oxford: Oxford University Press, 2018), 66-84.

[10]John Jefferson Davis, *Worship and the Reality of God: An Evangelical Theology of Real Presence* (Downers Grove, IL: IVP Academic, 2010), 90.

[11]Davis, *Worship and the Reality of God*, 110.

CONCLUSION

[1]Dietrich Bonhoeffer, *Psalms: The Prayer Book of the Bible* (Minneapolis: Fortress Press, 1974), 15.

[2]Bonhoeffer, *Psalms*, 14.

[3]John Updike, *Rabbit Redux* (New York: Random House, 2012), 245.